FOR FRYING OUT LOUD

REHOBOTH BEACH DIARIES

FAY JACOBS

Bywater
BOOKS

Ann Arbor
2016

Bywater Books

Bywater Books First Edition: May 2016

For Frying Out Loud: Rehoboth Beach Diaries
was originally published by
A&M Books, Rehoboth, DE in 2010

Cover designer: TreeHouse Studio

Bywater Books
PO Box 3671
Ann Arbor MI 48106-3671
www.bywaterbooks.com

ISBN: 978-1-61294-075-5 (print)
ISBN: 978-1-61294-076-2 (ebook)

To BJQ and the Usual Suspects

Table of Contents

I'm not a Delmarva native. Darn few of us here are. In fact, before I arrived I didn't know that Delmarva meant the Delaware, Maryland and Virginia eastern shore. Delmarvalous. Frankly, to be considered an old-timer you have to have arrived with the Dutch or been born in a manger in a chicken coop. So I'm an interloper. But that doesn't mean I don't love lower, slower Delaware.

Of course, when I first arrived, mid-1990s, everything was a culture shock for this New Yorker. Fresh off a daily one-hour commute, people here considered the one-mile ride from downtown Rehoboth to Route One going "all the way out on the highway." At best, a New Yorker might carve a pumpkin, but would never consider making one a prize-winning projectile like they do here at the Pumpkin Chunkin' Fest. Most tellingly, folks in Sussex mostly looked baffled when I mentioned Matzoh Ball soup.

As a matter of course, I was suspicious of any event celebrating live chickens or dead Horseshoe Crabs. And no bonafide New Yorker would ever be caught ordering a flat breakfast meat called scrapple made of spare pork parts too peculiar for sausage.

Sure, my real estate agent provided full disclosure that I was moving to Rehoboth Beach, but frankly it never occurred to me I'd be living in rural Delaware. The first time I ventured outside my comfort zone was to the DMV. At first I thought some patrons were civil war re-enactors but it turned out they were dressed for agribusiness. Who knew.

And people were really, really friendly, which made me both nervous and suspicious. I'd lived in a New York City apartment building for three years and never said a single word to anyone in the elevator. It's just not done.

My second expedition took me across the Woodland Ferry outside Seaford. I love a good ferry ride, like the one between Manhattan and Staten Island, crowded amid 30 vehicles and 4,440 passengers with, of course, nobody saying a word to each other. Twenty one million people ride it annually, racing five miles in 25 minutes, on the most reliable transit schedule in the U.S.

The Woodland Ferry, on the other hand, takes six cars and a sprinkle of chicken catchers over a really narrow trickle of the Nanticoke River. The slower lower trip, lasting five minutes, is like an arcade ride, and I love it. And it might or might not be running Thursday mornings because it might or might not be down for maintenance.

For sheer contrast with, say, Manhattan's Bloomingdales, we've got Wilson's General Store, and darn it, the shop was closed on the Sunday I first rode past. Their sign said Ammunition, Notary Public, Groceries, Meat, Hardware, Subs, and Coffee. You never know when you are going to need eggs and buckshot at the same time

I'm sure it surprises no one that prior to my first Apple-Scrapple Festival I was a scrapple virgin.

There I was, chowing down on this legendary farm food, negotiating it nicely until I looked up and saw the 40-foot scrapple company sign listing the ingredients as pig's snouts and lard.

Just then the Hog Calling Contest began with people wailing "Suuu-eeeee, Suuueeeee," which was roughly the same sound I was making spitting out my pig snout sandwich. Wisely my mate grabbed my arm and steered me toward a vendor hawking kosher hot dogs, which, if dissected, are probably the Hebrew National equivalent of snouts and lard.

Here's another of my favorite Sussex traditions – business cards by cash registers. Back in the Big Apple or its kissin' cousin downtown Rehoboth, business cards by the register represent realtors, day spas and concierge services. A mere mile outside town, there are cards for gun cleaning, taxidermy, and deer-cutting. So near and yet so far.

Hey, just last week I saw a wild turkey by the side of the road, recognizing it as such from my previous experience with a whiskey bottle. This turkey had an under-chin wattle just crying out for a good plastic surgeon. I was sure it was my find of the day until I passed the front yard with the camels in it. I imagine every day, not just Wednesday, is hump day in that household.

Then there's the infamous Delaware State Fair Duck Drop? Officials literally drop a duck (albeit gently) onto a numbered grid where people have plunked down money to wager which grid gets the first duck poop. You can't make things like this up.

We also have the prehistoric-looking horseshoe crab. They say it's more closely related to spiders, ticks, and scorpions than to crabs and I believe them. New York has its crustaceans, mostly on menus, but I can't remember ever seeing a horsehoe crab wash up on Fire Island. Here, in the name of eco-tourism, they throw the damn things a festival.

So my love affair with the coast and its rural neighbors continues. Not that I haven't shared my culture with the locals. Lots of long-time Delmarvans can be found singing karaoke with me to Liza's "New York, New York," spearing matzoh balls at my Passover Seder, or razzing me for my allegiance to the Bronx Bombers. Don't tell anyone, but lately I've been rooting for the Shorebirds, our local farm team.

But I do have to be careful. Last time I went to New York I inadvertently started chatting with people in an elevator and almost got myself arrested. I'm an honorary Delmarvan now. Except for the Scrapple. Some traditions are just too hard to swallow. ▼

January 2007

The terrorists have won. They've turned the once exhilarating adventure of airline travel into an excruciating ordeal. Between terrorists and Big Business, air travel is now an extreme sport.

I recently attended a conference in Seattle (and Bonnie came along, not realizing travel was no longer fun) and I have never, ever, had a worse travel experience, including the time my ass fell asleep on a 25-mile bike trip. (I know, what was I thinking?)

But the very act of getting from Philadelphia to Seattle without going insane was as extreme as it gets.

From the Al Qaida security handbook:

1. Liquids, gels and aerosols must be in three-ounce or smaller containers. Rolled up toothpaste tubes are forbidden. Is a terrorist likely to commandeer a plane by strapping himself with Crest Whitening gel?

2. Liquids must be placed in a single, quart-size, zip-top, clear plastic bag. I can't seal ziplocks correctly with leftovers in them, so you can imagine how well I do trying to zippity do dah in front of armed guards.

3. Each traveler must place their plastic, zip-top bag in a bin for screening. My shampoo gets an MRI and I get to toss my shoes, wallet, keys and phone into a bin and watch it get sucked into a black hole – while I step through the metal detector and get felt up by a security worker and her explosive detection device.

Those people have a tough job. If they're looking for sweaty, suspicious-acting terrorists, we're all sweaty and suspicious, praying we'll get our valuables back before somebody else does.

All this happens barefoot of course, ever since that goofy-looking schmuck tried to blow up a plane with dynamite in his shoes. Now we have to remember to spray Dr. Scholl's foot powder in the morning so we can get barefoot without causing a concourse evacuation.

I was relieved to read you can carry breast milk onto the plane. I've got to assume they mean outside the body. And all of a sudden tweezers are okay again. The Homeland Security police must have been confronted by an angry mob of menopausal woman threatening to grow goatees on long flights.

Yet, you'll be pleased to know that while a whole list of things are banned from carry-on luggage, it's perfectly alright to carry spear guns, meat cleavers and ice axes in checked luggage. Look around when you get your bags off the carousel; you could be standing next to a psychopath wielding a meat cleaver.

Once harried travelers emerge from the strip-search it's time to run to the gate. If you stop to gaze at the departure screen, don't take your hand off your luggage. Like the eternally looping announcement says, airport police can swoop in and detonate your unattended suitcase.

Hell, I am now forbidden from packing anything important anyway – just a magazine, my three ounces of toiletries and extra panties in case my checked luggage winds up some place other than I do. I can see them blowing up my carry-on and having to duck and cover from exploding underpants.

So we get onto the plane and immediately everybody heaves their carry-on up into the over-heads. Of course, the man ahead of us clogs the whole boarding process by trying to stuff a bag the size of a cello over my head. Hey, Pablo, check the damn thing.

Then we notice that despite paying $44 each to purchase five extra inches of leg room we're still crammed in like sardines. Umm, we actually are flying united.

Then we get to savor this experience longer than scheduled: the plane's A/C goes up and until they fix it we're stuck enjoying the five extra inches (is this sounding smarmy to you, too?) for 45 extra minutes, packed in a stifling aluminum tube.

Finally we are airborne and listening to the flight attendant's instructions for grabbing our seat cushion to use as a flotation device should the plane ditch in the water. Hell, bending my arm to reach under my butt would shatter my right elbow on the window and my left on Bonnie's jaw. I'd have to float as I'd never be able to swim.

More survivable might be an emergency landing on terra firma. But Bonnie turns to me and says "How can we get into the crash position? On the way to putting our heads between our knees we'll knock ourselves unconscious on the seat in front of us."

Actually, it might be easier to put our heads between each others...um, I'll stop now....

Then the flight attendant comes by with the beverage cart, but we're packed so tightly neither one of us can get to our wallets without breaking a rib. We settle for free Diet Coke. As I raise the four ounce cup of liquid to my lips the guy in front of me tilts his seat back slamming me in the tits with the tray table and shooting the soft drink up my sinuses. Now that's snorting coke.

Did I mention we had middle and window seats with (what else?) a Sumo wrestler on the aisle? But you knew that.

Finally, we land some place in America's heartland, 45 minutes late for a connecting flight where the layover was supposed to be 55 minutes.

We go running down the concourse, tickets, I.D.s and chins flapping, gasping for air, screaming from shin splints, racing to the gate. Mercifully that flight was delayed by, I don't know, sunshine? We made it by a whisker. Thank God I had the tweezers.

The second flight was, if possible, more painful than the first, since we hadn't sprung for extra leg room. By way of contrast, Bonnie and I exited Seattle on a scenic train heading for Vancouver BC. It left and arrived on time, had roomy, comfortable seats and a dining car serving a full breakfast. The friendly porters had a delightfully quaint manner and provided a startling level of service. We might have been on the Orient Express.

Sadly, we didn't have a week for Amtrak to take us home. Fro pretty much mirrored To. Only instead of a cello, a fellow passenger tried to stow what looked like a John Deere tractor in the overheads.

When I got home I happened upon the Extreme Sports Channel where they mentioned "a bunch of hardened riders busting their asses." I don't know what sport they were talking about but it could have been the 747 fuselage team.

Actually, I looked it up. An extreme sport is defined as any sport with a very high level of danger, often involving speed, altitude and a heightened level of physical exertion. Such activities induce an adrenaline rush and the outcome of a mismanaged incident may be death.

Now I realize that statistics say flying is far safer than driving. That may be true, but these days, the extreme sport of air travel is less likely to induce an adrenalin rush and more likely to induce a persistent vegetative state. Fortunately, the outcome of a mismanaged cabin incident may only be Diet Coke-covered clothing and inadvertent snuggling with strangers. But it sure ain't no fun anymore.

Next, I'm off to New Orleans for a publishing convention. Let the extreme games begin....

February 2007

If you've paid even the slightest bit of attention to the struggle for gay rights in this country you know of Barbara Gittings. You might not recognize the name, but you remember seeing photos, from 1965, of homosexuals, men in suits and ties, women in skirts, protesting for gay rights in front of the White House. Barbara was there, and she called it picketing. Most people call it the beginning of the entire gay rights movement in this country.

Barbara Gittings passed away too soon, on February 18 at age 75, after an incredibly courageous battle against breast cancer. She was a young 75, vigorous until close to the end, and passionate about her cause, probably until her last second of life. I've known of Barbara Gittings and her activist work almost from the moment I peeked my nose out of the closet in 1982, already more than thirty years into Barbara's very visible gay rights crusade.

And while I knew of her for years, I only got to meet her last summer. And only for one weekend. But it was a total immersion weekend, filled with astounding stories of early organizing, picketing, and the way things were.

For the way things are, we can thank Barbara and her partner of 46 years Kay Lahausen. They were tireless and achieved a great deal in our struggle for equality. We all owe them – big time.

When Delaware Stonewall Democrats planned their annual fundraiser last summer, they decided to honor two different parties. Their 2006 accolades were to go to Sarah and Jim Brady, for their wonderful spirit, local and national activism, and caring. The other honoree would be Gay rights pioneer Barbara Gittings.

We had heard she wasn't in the best of health, having fought cancer for years, and recently undergoing another course of chemotherapy. She told Stonewall organizers she was hesitant to make the drive from her home in Wilmington to the beach by herself, as her partner Kay had mobility issues and wouldn't be coming along. Bonnie and I volunteered to pick Barbara up on Friday night, transport her to Rehoboth and welcome her to our guest room.

From the minute she hopped (and it did seem like a hop) into our car, this petite and lively woman with the delightful smile started peppering us with questions. She wanted to know where we lived, how we met, what movies we liked, the last book we read, how many siblings we had, if we were out of the closet to relatives, and dozens more inquiries. For our part we answered, exchanged a lot of laughs, and heard much of her story, too. Two hours later, when our car turned off Route One onto Old Landing Road, we were behaving like three old friends.

Interspersed with the life stories, Barbara cautioned that she tires easily and might not be up for too busy a weekend. No problem, we said, our house is yours for resting, relaxing and whatever you need for the weekend.

"Where's the best place for dinner?" she asked immediately, "I love great restaurants. And can I meet some of your friends?"

While she disappeared into the guest room to change clothes, we invited four friends over for pre-dinner cocktails. When Barbara reappeared, she was wearing white tennis shorts, sneakers and a bright orange t-shirt with the slogan "Gay? Fine by Me!" on it.

Our friends arrived, I mixed martinis and Barbara sat cross-legged on our sofa, one of my dogs in her lap. She told us stories about her involvement in those White House pickets ("I insisted that we had to dress conservatively") and the early days of the organization Daughters of Bilitis – the first and most famous lesbian rights organization. We learned the inside story of her arranging for a gay psychiatrist, disguised to protect his identity, coming to speak at the National Psychiatric

Association. That event led directly to the 1973 NPA vote to remove homosexuality from their list of mental illnesses.

We offered Barbara a roster of Rehoboth restaurants and she selected a lovely upscale French place, for what turned out to be a fabulous dinner filled with great food, wine, and conversation.

After dinner, our guest asked if we could go to the boardwalk, so we drove up past the Henlopen Hotel, where we could access the beach and a great view of Rehoboth by night. "Can we walk?" Barbara asked. "Sure," we said, heading south along the boardwalk towards Rehoboth Avenue.

Then we passed the Avenue, continued walking under the stars toward Funland, and quickly, all the while chatting about politics, reached the end of the boardwalk.

"I'll go get the car," Bonnie said.

"No," said Barbara, "let's walk back. And get some caramel popcorn on the way!"

If our guest tired easily, there was no evidence that night, even as Bonnie and I huffed and puffed returning to the car.

Back at home, there was a message on the phone from Barbara's partner Kay, asking if we would please take photos of the next day's Stonewall event for their memorabilia collection.

The next day saw breakfast out, terrific stories, sharing of views, a little shopping at our gay bookstore and then the Stonewall event.

With perfect summer weather, and a large crowd, the stage was set for the big backyard event at the home along Silver Lake. A host of officials spoke, along with attending politicos, and finally we got to the honors. Both Sarah and Jim Brady, as well as Barbara made passionate and effusive remarks. Stonewall presented Barbara with a lovely glass bowl, which she excitedly held over her head for all to see as she challenged us to keep up the fight.

Following the cocktail hour event it was off to dinner again. This time Barbara chose a gourmet Asian restaurant where we had another wonderful meal and more animated conversation.

Bonnie and I were a little sad, because our weekend together was coming to an end.

On Sunday morning, Bonnie cooked pancakes as we sat around our table chatting about Rehoboth and Delaware politics. Then it was time to return Barbara to Wilmington. I don't think any of us wanted the weekend to end. As we drove North, Barbara wanted to know everything she had failed to ask us on the trip down and we wanted to know more about her career. It turns out that she and Kay mostly held low-level administrative jobs to fund their real jobs as gay rights activists. We realized all the things Barbara and her contemporaries went through to make our current lives here in Rehoboth possible.

When we dropped her off at home, we felt like we'd made a wonderful new friend and she promised to stay in touch as well.

Through September we exchanged a few e-mails, and I soon got a package – a wonderful autographed book full of interviews from the early gay rights activists and quite a bit about Barbara herself. She also told me to look for a new documentary in which she was interviewed. In exchange, I sent along the Stonewall event photos.

I was caught up in other things last fall – writing jobs, political races and putting the finishing touches on my next book. It was a while before I realized I hadn't heard from Barbara regarding the package of pictures.

And I was totally stunned and saddened last week when I heard she had passed away, with Kay at her side.

Bonnie and I were unhappy we hadn't gotten the chance to see Barbara again, but I was torn. Selfishly I'd rather remember her charging in and out of our house, curly grey hair askew, asking questions, laughing out loud and wearing her "Gay? Fine by Me!" t-shirt.

You're going to miss her whether you knew her or not.

March 2007

With an intolerant, bigoted boss like Chairman of the Joint Chiefs, General Peter Pace, why would a gay person even *want* a military career?

But gay people do. They want to serve their country and get an education. They are willing to slog through a hideous political blunder like Iraq, risking their lives, to do it.

And General Pace says they are not worthy of offering that sacrifice. It's a savage insult to gay citizens everywhere and some people are applauding him for it.

His reasoning isn't even as sly as the usual rant against gays in the military. The prevailing idiocy allows that gays would disrupt morale and discipline. In other words, gay people shouldn't be allowed to serve because straight people are scared of them. It's a sad and frequently offered argument.

But no, General Pace doesn't hide behind the *morale* issue. He deletes an "e" and declares it to be a *moral* issue. To his closed mind gays are not moral, therefore they should not serve.

I think he's hideously wrong of course, but in America he's entitled to his opinion. But since he's representing the entire U.S. military, I think he should be fired faster than a speeding Baghdad bullet. That's *my* exercise of free speech. It's indefensible that he wants his personal beliefs to govern public policy. Last time I checked we weren't a theocracy yet.

But at least General Pace is honest.

Bigots who hide behind the troop morale pretext make me gag. These people envision gay men who would choose military careers wearing nipple rings with their uniforms, soliciting in the showers and threatening the dignity of heterosexuals as they lie in their barracks beds. You just know that's what they conjure in their tiny intolerant brains.

Indulge me, but do you know any nudists? I do. At least I've heard that some people I know are nudists (or naturists as they prefer to be called). Since I'm not a naturist myself (I hear you breathing that sigh of relief) the world of naturism is foreign to me. Even a little off-putting, if you will, because I know nothing about it and it raises thoughts of a great big social taboo. Fine. While I'd be uncomfortable at a party with naturists behaving like naturists while I try to avert my eyeballs, I have no problem with naturists who are dressed in public. What they do behind closed doors or on secluded beaches is their business.

But if the aforementioned naturists worked at CAMP Rehoboth (they don't, so stop fantasizing) or in a corporate setting where they valued their careers, would they strip down and show me Trafalgar Square by the water cooler? Would they attend staff meetings in the nude? Not only wouldn't they do it, but where would they stash their Blackberrys?

Let's ask ourselves if America would put up with a public policy stating that naturists are barred from military service or corporate careers because they behave in an immoral manner in private? Sadly, now that I've brought the subject up, under the current political administration, they just might. But it would be unforgivably stupid, insulting, and a complete waste of talented people who would show up to work in clothing, even on casual Friday.

Okay, you can pick at this analogy, but in a hate-the-sin, love-the-sinner scenario, it's just as disturbing to bar gay people from the military when they are not having sex as it is to bar nudist people from the military when they are not butt naked.

Yes, I know, *practicing* nudity is a choice and *practicing* homosexuality is how we are born (besides, we don't need practice, we are good at it). And yes, I know that being a nudist is a choice and being a homosexual is not. But face it, if we apply the ridiculous hate-the-sinner standard to both, nudists and gays would be suspect for what they DO, not who they are.

I think it's ridiculous to bar homosexuals and nudists from the work place even when they are not practicing, in public, for all the world to ogle, the act that labels them homosexuals or nudists in the first place.

Ooh, here's another imperfect but illustrative analogy of naked is as naked does. While I may not be a nudist (sorry to remind you of that image again), I do have a tattoo. A small one, on my ankle. But years ago I knew a fellow who went into a tattoo frenzy in college. By the time I met him, he was reconciled to wearing long sleeves, even on sweltering days, just to look appropriate at client meetings. He may have been a proud tattoo owner on Friday evening, but during the work week he wore his corporate drag.

Would a person who wants to show off, all the time, tattooed arms, legs, and cheeks in both possible locations want to work in a place where everybody else covers up with Armani? I think not. Likewise it would be pretty brainless for a nudist to expect to be able to show up in the Board room without his pants.

So too, even pea-brained bigots have to realize that a gay man who wants to succeed in the military would not jeopardize his career by wearing a feather boa with fatigues or a tank top saying "You Go Girl" while he's in a tank.

I'm using the boys as an example here because we all know that the military would collapse without its lesbians. But the women who value keeping their jobs will behave correctly as well.

I say we judge everybody by the same behavior standard. There are disciplined gays and lesbians, nudists, and tattooed ladies and gentlemen along with the requisite few misbehaving naturists, tattooees, straight people and homos.

Let everyone who wants to serve do so. After that, go to town making sure everybody behaves appropriately for the military. What's so hard about that?

I'm so furious, that this tattooed gay gal wants to strip and moon the military, starting with General Peter Pace. Close your eyes, sir, I'm not kidding. ▼

April 2007

When I moved to Rehoboth full-time eight years ago, I thought I'd constantly be doing a reverse commute for Washington, D.C. weekends. How could I live without Thai food, theatres, museums, or national politics? I envisioned frequent caravans for culture.

Hasn't happened.

The Rehoboth I moved to already *had* gourmet restaurants, and more ethnicity soon followed. Rehoboth had live theatre and more has developed; many of our friends were already weekenders, with an astonishing number having made the move full time. And frankly, knowing that most people make their closest friendships early in life, I never dreamed I'd meet so many people and enlarge my circle of friendships so meaningfully here in Sussex County.

Oh, and the Rehoboth Museum is on the cusp of opening. It's not the Smithsonian, but it's ours.

Not feeling the pull to go West, as the Village People might sing, it's been a rare trip back to civilization.

Bonnie and I (and the dogs) made the drive to Maryland on a recent Friday to stay with friends, see *The Heidi Chronicles* at Arena Stage and enjoy D.C. in the spring.

Upon our arrival we walked the dogs through lush mounds of fallen Cherry Tree petals, and gazed with wonder at all the old-growth landscaping, bursting with bright red and pink azalea blossoms, Dogwood blooms and those ubiquitous and almost-but-not-quite-finished-blooming Cherry Trees.

On a driving tour we were gape jawed at Bethesda and Silver Spring, once sleepy diner-dotted suburbs, now morphed into towering urban metropoli. Asian fusion food, gobs of galleries, and behemoth Barnes & Nobles punctuated the cityscape.

Blues skies and a sunny day accompanied our winding drive down Rock Creek Parkway toward the D.C. waterfront, all the while passing the well-known architectural edifices devoted to our nation's history. Adjacent was the sparkling Potomac River, people in paddle boats and city streets bursting with activity.

I'm loathe to admit that I suffered a momentary pang – was it regret? – for leaving all this behind and running off to the Delaware beaches. Dare I say it? Had I erred? Could small town Rehoboth ever compete with *this*?

The Capitol Dome loomed, bright white against a perfectly blue sky, looking glorious in the humidity-free air. This was a perfect 10 for a Washington, D.C. day.

But Lo! What were all those clunky concrete barricades and big black fences? And Military Police with weapons? My God, the place was practically shouting "Code Orange!" for Homeland Security and our government buildings were cowering inside their own terrorist-proofed Green Zone. Security-blocked roads made navigation dicey on the way to the Maine Avenue seafood district. As the car whipped from Southeast to Northeast, around this circle and that, I started to long for my one tiny Rehoboth Avenue traffic circle, with its one bicycle cop in shorts and no AK47.

On-street parking eluded us so we entered an underground bunker offering $5 for the first hour and your 401K for the rest. The shiny quarters reserved for the Rehoboth meters were useless here; credit cards with increased limits encouraged.

Upstairs, the famed waterside seafood restaurant sprawled from dining room to dining room, with no less than five massive buffet stations offering deep fried, steamed, broiled, and sauced seafood, fried chicken, jambalaya, chowder, a beef carving station, copious salads, butter-drenched corn, moun-tains of caloric desserts and an entire buffet table devoted to breakfast blintzes, burritos, pancakes, and hominy grits.

The bounty could bring weight watchers to their knees, but it was all astoundingly mediocre – a word not associated with

Rehoboth eateries. Besides, for $25 per person at home we can have breakfast or lunch anywhere in town, stroll the boardwalk for a funnel cake dessert, buy a t-shirt, and still not top twenty five bucks a head.

In the interest of full disclosure, the matinee was pretty good. You can't beat the production values money can buy. But truthfully, although the cast had wonderful resumes, some of the shows I've seen at the beach have had more heart. That surprised me.

Heading out of the fortified Green Zone and the atmosphere of Martial Law, back to the slightly smaller city of Bethesda, we got tangled in traffic. Passing the tony Chevy Chase Metro I was astounded and saddened to see a homeless woman living in her own Green Zone of cardboard boxes right there at the station. Welcome to the big city.

Driving along Maryland and Virginia highways and past mature neighborhoods put my local concerns for overdevelopment in perspective. Maryland and Virginia are full, completely used up, every inch developed, like a Monopoly board. I realize that we've cultivated a huge crop of townhouses recently, but lucky for us we still have our chicken coops, rural roads and undeveloped waterfront. At least for now.

And Washington, D.C. doesn't have the Apple-Scrapple celebration and the amazing Delmarva Chicken Festival. Yes, I am claiming them as mine.

As for the Maryland Monopoly suburbs, every time we passed GO, in the shops or on the highways, it was time to pay $200 in sales tax and highway tolls – another reason to appreciate tax-free Rehoboth.

Sunday night. The pups had it with the leash thing and longed for their fenced backyard with its doggie door. I'd had enough of the traffic and hassles. On the city-bound lanes coming back from the beach, vehicles crept bumper to bumper with weekenders returning from the shore. On our side, it was clear sailing toward home.

Now I'm not saying that the lone Cherry Tree starting to

blossom on our lawn can hold a candle to Washington's Tidal Basin display, or the dwarf azaleas getting ready to bloom are worthy of a garden tour, but it's home sweet home to me. Without the armed guards or Homeland Security codes, thank you. Home. Land. Security. Ahhhhhh.▼

May 2007

The trouble began when I slowed down. I'm sure you've heard me whining about needing time in the slow lane. Well, Sunday was it.

In fact, the morning rain inspired me. I didn't put on my glasses until 1:30 in the afternoon and then, only to dial the phone to cancel plans. I didn't get out of my pajamas until 5 p.m., spending the entire day on the sofa with Bonnie, the dogs, the TV remote and a staggering assortment of junk food.

Sadly, immediately following *Face the Nation*, the television offerings turned into a wasteland. Between *Pet Stars* ("Let's welcome Hoagie the ping-pong playing pooch!") and *Shear Genius* (Hairdressers, rev your blow dryers!) Sunday viewing is not fit for (wo)man nor beast.

Sometimes it's not fit for man and beast – like the game show where contestants drop a ferret down their pants to clock how long they can keep the thing from crawling out their cuffs. You should see the screaming and clutching of clothing. By the ferret. Hey, big boy, is that a ferret in your pocket or are just you glad to…I could not possibly have made this show up.

In the midst of this ferret commotion, the incident happened. My 12-year old 27-inch television got the hiccups. The screen erupted into black & white squiggles accompanied by ear-splitting static.

I dropped the cheese doodles, unfolded myself from the sofa, the dogs, and my mate, marched over to the set and gave it a whack. Everything returned to normal, or as normal as it can be when you are watching a man with a ferret in his trousers.

Life was good for another hour or so (thankfully, we'd found a movie to watch), until the screen exploded into a purple haze, requiring me to disturb everybody again and go whack the idiot box.

By late in the day, I needed that product they are advertising ad nauseum *Head-On, apply directly to the forehead,* and the television needed a whack job every 15 minutes.

The inevitable conversation ensued. Do we see about fixing the TV or do we do what we really want and buy a big honkin' flat screen TV?

For a few minutes, Bonnie and I pretended there were two sides to the argument. Ultimately, we realized that neither of us was in physical shape to drag the monstrous antique TV into the car to seek medical attention. Also, TV repair persons went extinct so long ago we were still calling them TV repairmen.

Negotiations broke down so we went to bed. In the morning I talked to my friend the accountant, who generally doles out conservative financial advice. He said to junk the TV. After all, in two years, when Digital TV becomes the law of the land (ahead of, I'm sure, the Employment Non-Discrimination Law) our current TV will be obsolete.

Alrighty then. We went to the Sony outlet. "Just to look." I didn't believe that either.

Have you tried to buy a TV lately? You need a diploma in quantum electronics and the patience of a saint. Question One: LCD or Plasma? After a 50 minute lecture from a pimply teenager I still couldn't tell them apart, except that plasma would bleed my bank account. We chose LCD.

Next we had a choice of a set with 1029 interlaced pixels or 720 progressive pixels (I always lean toward the progressive), different aspect ratios, viewing angle specs, and something called a bit rate. I bit my lip and stared at the clerk like he had sprouted antennae.

"I want one with a black border," I said, hoping Bonnie could figure out the rest.

In the darkened display theatre I stood watching seven screens simultaneously show copulating moths while Bonnie listened to the salesperson drone on about color temperatures and video dithering. Meanwhile we dithered at Sony trying to keep our heads from exploding. (*Head–On, apply directly to the forehead*).

I awoke from my technology coma to ask "Do we just take one of these home and plug it in like a regular TV?"

"Just like a regular TV," said the adolescent clerk.

For the finale we had to deal with the size question. Did we size queens want a 32-inch or 40-inch flat screen LCD? Standing in the 8,000 square foot store, we were pretty certain the puny 32-inch was way too small.

Our first clue should have been the trouble the Sony kids had getting the box into the car. We drove it home minus the carton. Then, our second clue should have been the compulsory gymnastics routine we executed getting the appliance in the front door. But we dragged it inside and perched it where old reliable Mr. 27-inch (don't go there) once stood.

Whoa! TV, where you taking that living room?

Let's just say it looked like the I-Max landed in the confines, and I mean confines, of my little house. Aesthetically speaking, it was the TV that ate the room.

Recognizing my decorating dilemma Bonnie sensibly said "Well, let's sit down and watch something and then decide."

Righteeo. The thing had a gazillion inputs and outputs and peepholes and plug-ins. I wanted to stick the little Sony clerk into one of them. I'd never seen so many cables. An hour later Bonnie had accidentally enabled picture and sound simultaneously and we sat down to watch Anderson Cooper because by this time it was very late.

God, you could see each strand of his gorgeous silver hair and determine what color Max Factor foundation he'd used on his baby face. I should have been listening to news about the G8 Summit and all I could think about was whether Anderson should have had that lower front tooth capped. What? Mom Gloria Vanderbilt couldn't afford the orthodonture?

Omigod, political reporter Candy Crowley had a big zit on her chin. Next, on *Law and Order,* they were checking the blood spatter patterns in what seemed like my entire living room.

I LOVED the big screen picture.

My spouse then informed me we weren't even watching in High Definition yet.

For that pleasure we'd have to pay an extra $5 a month to Comcast. But more importantly, I'd have to wrestle down my aesthetic demons. How could I have a TV bigger than my cocktail table?

So did we go back for the measly 32-inch screen? No. For once in my life did I choose function over form? Yes. One look at a Dodge Durango commercial with wide-screen mountains narrowed my resolve. A bigger than life head shot of Sandra Bullock and I was cooked. So what if my living room looks like the RKO Multiplex.

Now I can't wait for Sunday to see those giant ferrets in humongous trousers. *Head-On, apply directly to the MasterCard.*▼

June 2007

Dammit, it happens annually. I get a year older.

Last year, on the morning of the anniversary of my birth, my cell phone rang. I answered and all I heard was a cat meowing the Happy Birthday song. The whole song. Then the cat hung up. I figured it was my sister, who lives in New York with way too many cats in a two bedroom apartment. Never did find out for sure.

I was still trying to place the timbre and tone of the meow mix when the phone rang again. This time is was a New York cousin, a wonderful Gay man, who proceeded to sing Happy Birthday to me in perfect Ethel Merman, followed by an encore of "There's Noooo Birthday Like Yourrrrr Birthday, Like Nooooo Birthday I Knooow…unique to say the least.

That same day I was talking with my father and I asked him "What were you doing 58 years ago today?"

"Same thing I'm doing now," he said.

What??? Pacing in the hospital? Watching a vaginal delivery? Drinking Johnny Walker?

"I'm yelling at the Yankees. They stink." Well, it's true, he's been hollering free advice to the Yankee manager of the moment for over eight decades. My father was listening to a game on the car radio on June 29, 1948 and missed my birth entirely. I anticipate a call from him on June 29 this year to wish me Happy Birthday amid his snarling at the Bronx Bombers.

I have a love-hate relationship with birthdays. I enjoy celebrating them. But actually having them is getting old, like me.

You know, I wouldn't mind turning 59 so much if it wasn't for all the bad news reports about Baby Boomers. This week alone I have read: "Achy baby boomers aren't aging gracefully. A wave of baby boomers may be hobbling toward retirement in worse health and with more aches and pains than people born…."

That's encouraging. Take two aspirin and call me in the....

And *Newsweek* had "The generation that vowed to stay forever young is coming up on a major milestone...they've been hippies and yuppies; and now it's the time of the 'abbies': aging baby boomers...." If the Beatles were still together would they be singing Abbies Road?

Web MD says "baby boomers are about to do something utterly conventional and predictable. They're going to start getting old and begin developing health problems. One big question looms over these developments: Will those years be vigorous and healthy, or will baby boomers sink into the pain and disability of chronic disease?"

Good god, by this time the Beatles would be singing "If I Fell" (and I can't get up) and "We can work it out" (on a Correctol commercial).

Auuuggghhh! Of course, if this health stuff isn't bad enough, the financial news is worse. Even the congressional budget office is weighing in. "Studies suggest that the average baby boomer's prospects for a comfortable retirement could face serious challenges."

Being in trouble on a personal level is bad enough, but the report continues with "Over the past 15 years, the retirement prospects of the baby-boom generation have become a source of public concern. Some experts contend that low saving by boomers could limit economic growth in the United States and compound the financial pressures that face government programs such as Social Security and Medicare."

Not only are we in danger of having less than financially secure retirements, we're going to be blamed for putting the federal government into financial chaos (like its not there already thanks to you-know-who, whose name I cannot even mention).

The survey also revealed that Baby Boomers have saved an average of only 12 percent of the total they will need to meet even basic living expenses in retirement. Twelve percent of my living expenses just about covers my bar bill. Cue the Beatles, hopefully, "All You Need is Love," because everything else will be too expensive.

And don't get me started about clothing. Trying to find attractive age-appropriate garments is like trying to find a drag queen at Nascar. All the fashionistas think they are doing a good thing by making trendy looking clothes in large sizes. Those huggy, midriff showing lacy things look great on Britney, Lindsay and Paris, but excessively stupid on Flopsy, Mopsy and size 16 Cottontail. Nobody wants to see a 59 year old belly button.

I did read that the fashion business is expected to under-go a "seismic mood swing" over the next few years in a trend they call "age-accepting" fashion – featuring more "realistic looking models, grey hair, and emphasis on empty nesting, retirement and widowhood in advertising."

Wow. That sounds like fun. Subscribe to the new magazines: *Harper's Bizarre*, *Done Housekeeping*, and *Ladies Rest-Home Journal*.

This is truly depressing. I'm working myself into quite a pre-birthday snit. I have to go have some ice cream. (She gets up from the computer.)

(She returns.)

Okay, I just looked at my June-July calendar. It includes several golf outings, dinner engagements, a pool party, four art openings, two book signings, a weekend of Broadway shows, a doggy play date with my pups and their friends, a ladies Tea Dance and goodness knows how many laughs.

Hell, growing old may be inevitable but growing up seems to be optional. And that's a good thing. Quoth The Beatles, "I'll Get By With a Little Help From My Friends."

Happy birthday Boomers....▼

GAY, GAY, GAY, GAY, GAY, GAY, GAY

Is there anything gayer than standing in front of the Stonewall Inn on Christopher Street in New York's Greenwich Village? I was there on Thursday, and never felt more gay. It felt good.

During Rehoboth's July 4th Fireworks, I listened to patriotic songs and desperately tried to separate them from the mess over at the U.S. Executive Branch, where Dick Cheney may or may not work (what does he do, have a desk on the Pennsylvania Avenue median?) and where W. just poked his finger in the eye of our entire Judicial Branch. Rehoboth may be Gayberry RFD, but by July 5th I needed a great big dose of Urban Gayboys and that Isle of Lesbos off the East River.

Get thee to Manhattan and the 14th Street B&B where we checked into a room adorned with a six foot head shot of Audrey Hepburn. Pretty darn gay.

If that wasn't enough, I read through the B&B welcome letter and noted that the special security code to get you in the door if you forget your key is Judy Garland's real name. That's so gay, in the very best sense of the popular phrase.

In fact, it reminded me how the Stonewall riots really happened. It wasn't particularly political or born of a well-oiled plan. It erupted because after Judy Garland's funeral that morning a contingent of gay fans and drag queens went to the Stonewall Inn to drown their sorrows. When cops raided the place for the umpteenth time that month, those queens rose up and said "not tonight, Josephine" or words to that effect and the bottle throwing began. On that hot, humid day, June 28, 1969, a lot of sad, soulful mourners turned into pissed off queens and kicked some serious police butt. Some say the uprising really launched the entire gay rights revolution. It's a daunting history for an unpretentious looking watering hole.

From that historic monument we strolled up Christopher Street to the Oscar Wilde Bookshop, the City's only exclusively

LGBT bookstore. I was delighted when the proprietor instantly greeted me by name even though I looked tubbier and more disheveled than I do on my Photoshopped book cover. Oscar Wilde is a great bookstore and, like other independent bookstores, is having a tough go of it.

Suppertime found us uptown dining with an old friend of mine and his husband. I *love* writing: "*his* husband or *her* wife." Those word combos are starting to sound natural. I remember being blown away reading an obit which referred to the deceased being survived by "his husband." Way to go, *Newsweek*, but after all, the couple lived in Boston, where same-sex marriage is legal.

My dinner companions ordered très gay cocktails (Manhattans, Cosmos, and Kir Royals) along with a fine meal and non-stop dish. And by "dish," I mean several yummy courses and nonstop gossipy gay chatter.

Then there was Broadway. The Great Gay Way. My reputation as a show queen is often at odds with my lesbian credentials. I adore those Broadway divas along with the boys, and I admit (just a bit embarrassed) that I would rather be in the third row cheering for Audra McDonald or Chita Rivera than Melissa Etheridge.

As for 4-time Tony Award winner Audra, we saw her give a stunning performance in *110 in the Shade*, a dusty, creaky old musical made splendid by her electric performance. Theatre queens from the balcony to the orchestra stood and shouted "Brava!"

Friday night found us seeing *Grey Gardens*, which just as easily could have been called *Gay Gardens*. It's gayer than *La Cage Aux Folles*. Not in the literal sense, but this musical, fashioned from the cult documentary film about lesser Kennedy relatives (Jackie's Bouvier cousins) living in squalor in East Hampton, fairly screams "gay!"

Mary Louise Wilson stars as nutty Edith Bouvier Beale and Christine Ebersole as her daughter Little Edie, a walking fashion police violation with delusions of sanity. Singer wannabe Edith's bachelor piano accompanist would have made Noel Coward look butch. You should have seen the boys lining up to give homage at the stage door.

It was great seeing Wilson again. I last saw her on stage playing the Stripper Tessie Tura to Angela Lansbury's Mama Rose in a 1974 production of *Gypsy*. Why do I know these things but cannot remember my computer passwords? Oh, right. I'm a gay man trapped in a lesbian's body.

And speaking of Lansbury, we saw her on Saturday night in *Deuce*, an anemic play about two aging tennis stars, where she played opposite Marian Seldes. Here's another gay connection–Marian played the long-time partner of Vanessa Redgrave in a brilliant but heartbreaking one act play televised as part of the movie *If These Walls Could Talk* several years ago.

But Angela Lansbury is royalty. To most folks she's that busybody from *Murder, She Wrote*, but theatre queens worship at her feet for her bitchy turns in the films *Gaslight* and *The Manchurian Candidate* and her Broadway musical comedy triumph in *Mame*.

And if all that isn't gay enough, she's done Sondheim. Enough said.

Deuce was nothing more than a vehicle for two legendary actors (there are no actresses anymore; my adoptive gay son informs me that we're supposed to call them all actors, but frankly I'm more used to saying "his husband" than calling Angela Lansbury an "actor") and it shows these two tennis stars pondering their careers, regrets, and relationships (not Sapphic, but that didn't stop them from talking about the lesbians on the courts and in the locker rooms). To say the play was a gay old time would not be a stretch.

Also during our long weekend we visited the Museum of Modern Art – inextricably gay. Dozens of male couples held hands as they browsed among Picasso (not gay), Van Gogh (did he have a thing for Gaugan?) and Andy Warhol (see title of article).

We dined at the new museum restaurant called Modern (not an innovative title, but an exquisite establishment) and three quarters of the incredibly attentive staff was surely gay.

Wrapping up the weekend, we visited New York's LGBT Community Center on 13th Street, which was in the thralls of celebrating a $9 Million grant from the City of New York to kick off their capital expansion program. The funding came from the Mayor and City Council. Oh my. Would that something like that could happen here at home.

By Sunday we piled our gay selves back in our gay car (Diesel for diesel dykes) and headed south toward Delaware's Oz.

If you are in the mood, New York can surely be all gay, all the time. In today's political climate it's good to have a total immersion gay experience every once in a while. It reminds us to be out, loud and proud.

And you don't really have to go to the Big Apple to experience it. In fact, when we pulled back into town, there was disco music emanating from any number of establishments in the community, with gaggles of guys and gals all over.

I'm as much for integration of gay and straight as the next person, but you know, it's great to retreat into an all-gay space every once in a while, if only to gather strength to fight for our rights.

Like little Frances Gumm (that would be Judy Garland) once said, there's no place like….▼

A WHOLE LOTTA UGLY
FROM A WHOLE BUNCH OF STUPID

I was wrong. Very, very wrong.

Recently, a controversy has been raging over the new musical film version of the fairly new Broadway musical of the old non-musical film version of *Hairspray*. Who says America doesn't recycle?

For the vehicle that began as an edgy John Waters movie, then made a huge splash on Broadway and is now at your local multiplex, it's been quite a ride. But following an opening shot from the *Washington Blade*, which seeped into the nation's blogosphere, there has been a dispute between a variety of gay spokespeople, official and otherwise, over the casting of John Travolta as Edna Turnblad in this latest *Hairspray*.

The Blade editor wrote that gays should boycott the movie specifically because Travolta is a Scientologist. Responding, John Waters defended Travolta as a joy to work with, a fantastic actor, and not in any way anti-gay.

(Disclaimer: I think Travolta has done some pretty decent film work, but his connection to Scientology, with their much publicized intolerance toward gay people and prescription medications bothers me and tars and feathers Travolta in my eyes. Then there's the maybe-he-is-or-maybe-he isn't-a homo aura to his personal life. But neither the actor's acting chops, nor his choice to stay in the closet if he is a homo, plays much of a role in my feeling about this particular dispute.)

The Travolta clash morphed from a discussion of whether a Scientologist should play Edna, to a secondary dispute regarding the history of the story and the gender of the actor who has, in the past, been cast as rotund Edna Turnblad. Edna is rotund Tracy's mother, and Tracy dances her way into the hearts of 1960s Baltimore and simultaneously manages to integrate the town.

If you are not a *Hairspray* groupie, in the original John Waters film Edna was played by portly drag queen Divine, who starred in Water's early, really edgy, well, very edgy, kinda disgusting films.

But 1998's *Hairspray* introduced Divine (and Rikki Lake as Tracy) to all manner of mainstream households through Waters' very sweet movie. It was funny, had a message, and no one did any of the revolting things they did in the earliest Waters' films. (Google *Polyester* or *Pink Flamingos*). One of Waters' films was called *Pecker*, and despite its nasty title was a charmer. I adored writing a review with the headline "I loved John Waters' *Pecker*."

Following in Divine's considerable footsteps came iconic gay actor Harvey Fierstein to play Edna in the Broadway musical *Hairspray*. He was fat, raspy-voiced and absolutely charming as Edna, with his gay icon pedigree adding to the excitement.

While nothing in the *Hairspray* script ever says Edna is a drag queen, and nothing is intended to denote any homosexual storyline, the original film and subsequent musical always had an elusive gay sensibility.

Although Harvey Fierstein readily admits he was just playing the role of a woman, much as Travolta said he was doing in a recent interview, lots of folks have their knickers in a knot because the casting of Travolta robs the new film of its undocumented and somewhat ethereal gay sensibility.

Originally, because of my admitted prejudice against Mr. Travolta and partially because I didn't spend much time thinking about the subject, I too, was pissed that Harvey or another out-of-the-closet actor was overlooked for the new *Hairspray* in favor of the *Grease*-y Travolta.

Well, I was wrong, wrong, wrong.

I saw the movie last night and I am still smiling. Travolta is a very sweet, exceptionally funny Edna.

More importantly, whatever gay sensibility was lost to casting is still alive and well everywhere in the film. Yes, the story is about racial prejudice in the 1960s and yes, yes, yes,

Tracy scandalizes the town by integrating not only the barely fictitious *Corny Collins* TV show (Baltimoreans, remember the *Buddy Dean Show*?) but all of a barely fictitious Baltimore as well. Tracy manages this by socializing with her "African American" friends. I use the quotation marks because in the film, Corny Collins allows those friends to dance on his TV show once a month for Negro Day.

At the film's first mention of Negro Day, there was a palpable sense of embarrassment in the theatre. If people didn't actually suck air, their faces felt hot as they remembered how horribly this country treated African Americans just a short time ago. Of course, I wouldn't call our nation's current race relations hunky-dory (or should I say honky-dory?) but at least it's no longer acceptable to openly discriminate – and the U.S. Government no longer officially codifies prejudice with state-sponsored discrimination against African Americans.

But wait! In exactly the same way as the citizens and government maltreated African Americans in *Hairspray* (and for real) gays and lesbians are now being maltreated.

Ba-da-bing! This movie has gay sensibility written all over it.

Trust me, the musical is hilariously funny, with great choreography, joyous music, and laugh outloud comedy schtik. There are awesome performances from the entire cast, including a surprise turn from Michelle Pfeiffer. Attention lesbians: if you swooned over her as she slithered across the grand piano in *The Fabulous Baker Boys*, her character here is not as alluring!

But apart from the terrific entertainment, the truth is, when I saw a candlelight march on screen, led by Queen Latifah and John Travolta, it was hard not to think, for just a minute, about that San Francisco vigil after Harvey Milk was shot, and the one in Wyoming after Matthew Shepard died. It reminded me of the marches we have made along Pennsylvania Avenue, chanting for our rights.

Hairspray is about intolerance, and since gays are the current and officially sanctioned piñata for intolerant people, I can only hope for a day when we get our *Hairspray* moment.

I want people in a movie theatre to get queasy, flinching when they hear how inequitably the nation treated gay people back in 2007.

As the inimitable Queen Latifah explains to a white teenager and her black boyfriend, "You've got to get ready to face a whole lotta ugly from a whole lotta stupid."

Well I'm afraid that gays are going to face a lump of ugly from a gang of stupid in the 2008 elections. I'm praying for an enlightened victor. And I hope our wait for equality and tolerance doesn't take more than half a century.

But in the meantime, let that Saturday night fever overtake you and go see *Hairspray*. You'll smile from start to finish, laugh a whole lot and feel good all over when the lights come up. It's great to watch a whole lotta stupid get their just rewards. ▼

August 2007

So, how do *you* feel today? I felt pretty good until I got my hands on some advice to extend my life.

Let me put forth a disclaimer here: I believe in traditional Western medicine, but I am also open to, although I haven't experienced much of, what folks call alternative therapies. From trigger point massage to acupuncture, natural remedies to yoga, I believe there are some great ideas and great practitioners around. And I mean absolutely no offense with the following...but...

Auuughhhhh!!!!!! I have just had the living poop scared out of me by a magazine purported to represent life extending alternative medicine therapies, regimens, drugs, machines and pills the size of bagels.

I sat down to warn you about this stuff just after I tried to swallow something that promised to extend my life. By the time I got finished choking the thing down, chasing it with water, then tomato juice, then a slice of cheesecake (it was the only edible in the fridge at the time), I'd used up twenty minutes of my life and clotted my arteries sufficiently to take two months off my existence at the other end.

Between the taste of the pill and the feeling that there's still a major league baseball stuck in my throat my life extension adventure is off to a rocky start.

It all started when my spouse went to have a treatment by our local Myofascial Trigger Point Therapist. Contrary to how it sounds, Myofascial does not mean a massage for your face. It's a discipline to treat muscle pain by finding the trigger points where the pain originates. Frankly, that means that the therapist sticks her elbow in the small of your back, trying to shove it through to your belly button so your rib cage will stop hurting. Honest. I've had treatment myself, for (I love saying this) a sports injury (stop laughing). It works and works well.

So my mate was behind closed doors having her triggers popped and I picked up a magazine we shall call Live Longer Than Most People. That's not the name, but I don't want litigation. I took the magazine home with me. Purportedly, this magazine features alternative meds and natural remedies to fix everything you can possibly die from, now or in the future.

In ten minutes I learned that I have to improve the endothelial function in my arteries, better absorb Bio CoQ10 for anti-aging, take Mitochondrial Energy Optimizer, eat pomegranate supplements, use Theanine to calm my nerves, avoid benzodiazepines (eek, don't step on the benzodiazepines), avoid the wrong form of Vitamin E (of course, that's what I take), swallow more butter extract, and keep from microwaving myself with my TV or cell phone. And I was just on page 32 of 94, not including the Buyers Club pages in the back.

The thing is, each article makes sure you know exactly which unhealthy pharmaceutical company drug is bad for you and tells you exactly which of their natural house brands MUST take its place or you are toast. The hell with Valium, Lipitor or soap and water. You have to use Reversatrol, Sesame Lignans and Olive Fruit Extract. Frankly, I get plenty of olive fruit extract from martinis.

From what I can glean from the articles and ads, if you take one pill from the greedy pharmaceutical companies, you have to replace it with four pills from the greedy Live Longer Than Most People people.

If you take even a small portion of their advice, you'd be in the bathroom every morning swallowing pills until lunchtime. If I do live twice as long but spend months at a time gulping handfuls of anti-mutagenic pills, is this a good trade-off? If I have to live like this I want my life to be shorter than most people.

Then there was the cautionary article "Single Fast Food Meal Increases Blood Pressure." I'm sure that's true. It should have been followed by "Single reading of this magazine monumentally increases blood pressure."

I turn the page. Look out for free radical reactions! I'm having a pretty radical reaction to this whole thing. Know what an adaptogen is? It's an agent that strengthens the body's response to stress. I think a stopreadingogen can do the same thing.

Then come the machines. Blood testers, capsule filler machines, Dr. Fung's Tongue cleaners (ick), pill grinders, and a Gauss Meter to detect radiation from my phone, photocopier and (omigod) my computer. Hell, I should be dead by now. Did you know that premature labor is associated with gum disease? While I don't have to worry about that, or the boswellia plant providing optimum prostate health, I can avoid some ugly maladies by using Live Longer Than Most People Toothpaste.

The magazine also recommends diets, all of them based on starving yourself to death. The Ultra Low Calorie Diet is, essentially, not eating. My idea of ultra low calorie is pizza minus the pepperoni.

The UltraSimple Diet advocates getting rid of extra body fluid. I do that already, after several Yuengling Lagers.

In the back of the magazine readers are invited on a special Live Longer Than Most People Cruise. You travel to the tropics while enjoying anti-aging lectures, Live Longer Than Most People gift baskets, and "insider secrets to significantly extend your life span." Wow, does the midnight buffet include all-you-can-swallow capsules, pills and Pomegranate Oils? Nightly in the lounge, Miracle Cures trivia? Excursions to Island health food stores?

There's even a Live Longer Than Most People Credit Card, with Merchandise Rewards. Don't ask. But you don't get Longer Than Most People to pay.

And on just about every page in this magazine there's a question.

LLTMP Magazine: Are you overdosing on Lipitor?

FJ: In their view, yes.

LLTMP: Can you manage stress without drugs?

FJ: Probably not.

LLTMP: Are you swimming in radiation emissions?

FJ: Absolutely.

I can't decide if I should go to the emergency room or suck down olive fruit extract at Happy Hour. I'm heading to the kitchen to finish the rest of the cheesecake so I can get my butter extract. Ahhhhh.…▼

August 2007

You may have read my previous rant about a cross-country flight that set a new low in comfort and customer service. While I didn't think it possible, that terrible record has been bested. Seattle to Philly had nothing on Philly to New York.

My step-mom Joan visited Rehoboth from New York last weekend. Since we didn't want Joan driving the distance alone, we suggested a short flight from White Plains, NY to Philadelphia, where we would pick her up. I'd taken that very same round trip in reverse last June and apparently there was a glitch in the system because both flights were on time and without incident.

Here, the similarity ends. When leaving N.Y., Joan's one-hour flight was more than three hours late. Apparently, somewhere in the continental United States, there had been weather.

On the following Monday, after a wonderful weekend, Joan and I headed back to Philadelphia for the departure leg of the journey. Leaving the car in Short Term Parking, we foolishly figured it might cost me "first half hour $4" but I'd certainly be back before it doubled, right? Yeah, you know.

We crossed from the parking lot to the departure area and discovered we were at U.S. Air Terminal B and not U.S. Air Express, Terminal F. However, a woman behind the ticket counter, said, "You can take a bus to your terminal, but we'll check your suitcase here." For a minute I considered sending Joan on the baggage belt with her suitcase.

I was heaving the bag onto the scale when another, quite frantic employee rushed at us whispering, "NO! Don't do it! We're having baggage issues!" Wow I'm glad I didn't plunk my family member down on that conveyor belt.

We snatched the bag from the jaws of defeat and schlepped it with us toward the shuttle bus to Terminal F.

The ride was so long I thought we'd accidentally gotten

onto the bus to Manhattan. But it finally delivered us to the very last door in the entire six-terminal airport, a good 5K from Short Term Parking. A few more yards and we'd have been in center city Philly with the Liberty Bell.

In the right place at the right time at last, we stared at the Departure screen, found the flight number and saw the throbbing words CANCELLED. CANCELLED. It sounded so, well, final. Joan and I exchanged helpless glances and headed for the ticket counter.

"Our flight's been cancelled, what now?" I asked.

"You wait," the agent said, dismissively.

"How long?" I questioned.

"Until we can get you on another flight. Looks like 4:30," he responded, head down, willing us to vaporize.

"Will I be able to get a refund if I drive to Amtrak at Wilmington instead?" I asked.

"Nope," said the dope, "our obligation is just to get you on the next available flight. And that's 4:30. But you can check your bag now."

I looked around to see if another employee was going to freak out and throw herself in front of the scale to stop me from checking the bag. No crisis worker intervened, so we watched the suitcase go bye-bye.

"Can I ask why the flight was cancelled?" I inquired.

"Operational Decision."

Really? They decided not to operate? Who's decision was this? Granted, there can't be throngs of people anxious to suffer modern day air travel for a measly one hour pain ride, so the flight must have been cancelled due to a masochist shortage.

I sighed and prepared to move on. But Joan, having stood demurely and quietly this whole time, addressed the agent.

"Aren't you even sorry?"

Way to go, Joan. The pompous, patronizing ticketing agent in this, the City of Brotherly Love, stammered some kind of answer as we turned and left. On our exit we spied a bank of "Courtesy Phones." I bet not.

That the next flight was just under five hours away was awful enough, but thanks to any number of terrorist threats, our airports are now hermetically sealed. No one without a boarding pass can enter any part of the airport where they dispense books, souvenirs, food or, as was becoming increasingly attractive, something to drink.

"Let's take that shuttle back to the Marriott at Terminal A," I suggested. We stood at the curb, waving, and a bus flew past without stopping. We flagged another and it too, whooshed by as if we were lepers. Turns out the shuttle only goes one way. Getting back from F to A is not their problem.

So we hiked the U.S. Air Express 5K, in the ninety degree weather. As it happens, every terminal from F to A had a wall-mounted Automatic External Defibrillator, just in case. Airport humor?

We crossed the Marriott finish line, with both of us schvitzing, panting and in serious need of adult beverages. Luckily, the restaurant was cool while we tried to get calm and collected. Spending a few extra hours together was a lovely gift, but it galled us to realize we'd be approaching New York's skyline by now if we'd just kept driving.

After a deliberately leisurely lunch, we boarded the shuttle yet again and headed for effing Terminal F. Although it was only 2:30 p.m., Joan opted to go through security to the gate so she could finish a book and I could get home. Naturally, some of her reading time was chewed up creeping in line for the X-ray machines, going barefoot, getting searched and generally being treated like a woman with explosives in her brassiere.

Concurrently, I dragged myself, amid further rising temperatures, back to the parking lot. En route I spied an air-conditioned van with the words Homeland Security Working Dogs on it. I longed to crawl in among the pack for a cool nap. With airport security at Code Orange I'd be quite willing to help sniff luggage. Finally back at short-term parking, where I had been for so long that my short term memory failed and it took me twenty minutes to locate my car, I had to pay an astronomical ransom for my vehicle.

With rush hour approaching, traffic crawled, my patience ebbed and I was still outside Smyrna, DE at dinner time. Hell, I could have been to New York, had a knish, and been back again by this time.

As it turned out, Joan's plane didn't leave Philly until after 5 o'clock, making this a record seven hour wait for a one hour ride. And, she arrived in New York to discover that – ta da! – her luggage didn't. I wish I'd had money on that. It was Tuesday before her bag finished its vacation.

So this is air travel 2007, brought to you by a merger of Corporate America and Jihad terrorists: F.U. Airlines Inc. Together they've replaced Fly the Friendly Skies with Apocalypse Now. Fasten your seatbelts. We're in for a bumpy time.▼

ATTENTION MELTING POT: GAY IS A CULTURE

Recently I had an incredible opportunity. The *Advocate* magazine published its 40th Anniversary edition, and on the cover was a photo collage of 40 of the most influential gay rights activists of all time. What a gift this is for our archives.

I say that, because I'm worried about losing our gay culture.

Do you agree that Gay is a culture? Just host a dinner party with seven gay people and a straight man or woman. It's a good bet that dozens of the evening's references, not in serious gay rights discussion, but casual conversation will buzz right over the outsider's head.

Not to say that inviting your straight friends to dinner is a faux pas. Au contraire. I wouldn't want to live in a ghetto, would you? That's why I love living in Rehoboth, with its diversity – and by this I mean a vibrant straight community along with us homos.

It's just that words or phrases like Stonewall Dems, show queen, "of course she bought a Subaru," and the ubiquitous "Did she bring a U-Haul on her second date?" are all in our lexicon and consciousness. It's our culture.

Judy Garland, Daughters of Bilitis, HRC, Billie Jean King, *Rubyfruit Jungle*, Drag Kings, Harvey Milk, P-Town. Our history, our heroes, our catch-phrases, our culture.

And I'm worried.

Exactly a decade ago writer Daniel Harris wrote *The Rise and Fall of Gay Culture*, a terrific discussion of those secret signals and shared sensibilities that allowed an underground gay society to flourish even as the larger population despised and discriminated against it.

The very act of showing up at a Judy Garland concert and seeing other gay men around the room, all sharing the vulnerability of Judy's music together made that denigrated community feel less alone.

But even a decade ago, Harris worried that assimilation and acceptance of homosexuals by society at large would cause our gay culture to disappear. It's the very same concern that different ethnicities, immigrants and religious sects have as they meet the great American, and now great global, melting pot.

But it seems to me that gay people often don't recognize gay as a culture. They do, of course, appreciate all the hard work that our gay pioneers did for the fight for gay rights in order to make their lives better. We're not ingrates. But I'm not sure our community sees our heroes, safe havens and that elusive quality called "the gay sensibility" as something to learn about and celebrate. And I think that's a shame.

While I've been mulling this over for quite a while, it really hit home this summer at female impersonator Christopher Peterson's show. While Christopher always receives cheers and ovations, I often saw blank faces on young gay people who really didn't "get" Bette Davis, mentions of *All About Eve*, or the importance (and I really believe this, *importance*) of Judy Garland to our community.

While Christopher does dead-on illusions of Bette Midler, Reba McEntire and others, I think our culture suffers if young gay people don't learn about early gay icons and cultural landmarks. Okay, I know I'm an old fart lesbian and many of these things were OF my generation. But many were not.

There's a terrific book by Delaware author Marcia Gallo called *Different Daughters* which tells the story of the lesbian rights organization The Daughters of Bilitis, which began to raise lesbian visibility in the tragically closeted 1950s and '60s. The name of the group came from a story by the poet Sappho, and the late lesbian activist Barbara Gittings always laughed and admitted that Bilitis sounded like a disease.

But the story told in Gallo's book is fascinating and inspires wonderment at the willingness of our foremothers to fight for lesbian visibility and rights when it was terribly dangerous to do so.

Every woman sipping beverages, listening to the music of the very talented Rehoboth singer Viki Dee and dancing at happy hour really should know about Del Martin, Phyllis Lyon, Barbara Gittings and Kay Lahausen, the aliases they had to use, and the crazy, determined chances they took.

If I'm being intolerably preachy here, I don't mean to be. But I was fascinated to learn that Bayard Rustin, an African-American gay man, was the organizer of the 1963 March on Washington with the famous "I Have a Dream" speech by Martin Luther King. He was drummed from the activist ranks because of his sexuality. I was captivated by the tale of Harvey Milk's rise to the title of *Mayor of Castro Street*, and was mesmerized learning how writer Lillian Faderman rose from indigent sex worker to revered professor of lesbian studies and continues to be an influential writer today.

Our schools teach Americans about Thomas Jefferson, Betsy Ross and American social history – the rise of the railroads, the Gold Rush, the McCarthy Era. And if we don't get it in school, I know that my Jewish parents handed down their culture and my friends of Italian heritage learned their stories from their families too.

It's a sure thing that heterosexual parents of gay youth are not teaching their kids homosexual culture! Lucky are our young gay people with two mommies or two daddies.

Gay people have to learn our history and culture on our own. There are hundreds of books available at our independent bookstores (although they are quickly disappearing), at the big chains and on line. And there's a wonderful lending library at CAMP Rehoboth if you want to know more.

I do.▼

November 2007

Since this is the last edition of *Letters from CAMP Rehoboth* for 2007 (where the hell DOES the time fly to?) I feel it's fitting to reflect on the year with some awards. Heck, everybody else does it. Whoopi and Hugh Jackman are booked so I'm presenting the awards myself. I promise to change t-shirts at least three times. The awards, in keeping with my literary theme, are the *Fry Babies*, for the things that got me frying in 2007.

Hope you don't mind, but I've cut the tacky opening production number (which had the cast of *Hairspray* singing and dancing "Come Fry with Me,") so we can get right down to business.

The envelopes, please.

The **Best Tap Dance Award** goes to Senator Larry Craig of Idaho, for his airport bathroom production number, playing footsie with a cop and proving, once again, that the most rabid anti-gay legislators are often found cowering in the closet but having sex in public. And Larry, you got additional points for suggesting that your foot wandered into the next stall so you could retrieve a fallen piece of toilet paper. That's just disgusting. Go wash your hands and wash your mouth out while you are at it. I don't know where it's been, but I can imagine.

Similarly, the **Do As I Say, Not as I Do Award** goes to the dishonorable GOP Senator David Vitter for admitting he patronized DC area prostitutes as well as working girls in his home district down South. As another legislator who regularly rants against gay marriage, methinks he's the one who is single-handedly (who knows, he may have used two hands) defiling the sanctity of marriage.

The **J. Edgar Hoover Red Dress Award** goes to Presidential Candidate Rudy Giuliani who has disavowed all support for his gay friends and their equal rights. I guess he's forgotten just how many unattractive photos of himself in drag

45

have been printed in New York newspapers over the years. Now I'm not intimating that Rudy is, in any way, gay. Only a straight man could enrage two ex-wives with his serial divorce antics. (Oh, wait, I'm forgetting about New Jersey's ex-Governor McGreevy...) Well, Rudy ain't gay. But he sure loves to play dress up.

The **Three Ring Circus Award for Homeland Security** to Ft. Lauderdale Airport staff for clearing a man through security and onto an airplane with a monkey smuggled under his hat. The flight attendant discovered the Marmoset sitting on the back of a seat when she came through to offer it a complimentary beverage. The security folks must have been busy looking for Republicans tap dancing in the bathrooms.

The **Things Go Better with Coke Award** to Lindsay Lohan, representing all the starlets who are trashing their reputations and blowing through their careers (no pun intended) when other deserving actors who would value their reputations don't get a shot. Just because she starred in *Herbie Fully Loaded* doesn't mean she has to walk around that way. The woman actually entered rehab as a PR stunt. Didn't she get the Anna Nicole memo?

The **Road to Hell Award** to DelDOT for consciously but unconscionably starting Rehoboth's Route One construction in August so they could be finished by June. What were they thinking??? Around here, August is worth two Junes. There are people who set out for the beach in August who are living in Smyrna now because that's as close as they could get.

The **Unabomber Anti-Technology Luddite Award** to Delaware's Sussex County Council for not encouraging homeowners to conserve energy by installing windmills in their blustery back yards. Energy-saving companies are partnering with energy conscious homeowners and their requests to install residential windmills have been turned down. It happened to my neighbors and we're going to be next. There's so much hot air in my backyard you'd think I'd been pontificating on the porch.

The **It Would Be Funny if It Didn't Hurt So Much Award** goes to President Bush and the Culture of Corruptions (great name for a boy band). They block kid's health care, help the insurance lobby provide us with crappy private coverage, then decry the evils of Socialized Medicine – all while enjoying free, government provided doctors appointments and trips to the government pharmacy for free Viagra (see first two awards). If that's not a well-functioning system of socialized medicine I'm the uncle of that monkey who boarded the plane in Florida.

The **New Orleans Gumbo Dumbo Award** to FEMA for staging a fake news conference about the California fires and asking fluff ball questions like "Is FEMA doing a heckuva job here or what!?" Their own staff asked glowing questions and gave glowing answers in a post-apocalyptic FEMA attempt at looking competent in an emergency. We want Brownie back....

And finally, the **Give Me a Reason It's not Treason Award** (also known as the **Go Take a Leak Award**) goes to Lewis "Scooter" Libby, former chief of staff to Vice President Cheney, found guilty of obstruction of justice and perjury for outing CIA agent Valerie Plame. All smarmy obfuscation tactics aside, Mr. Libby, as fall-guy for Rove, Cheney, et al actually aided and abetted the enemy by outing Plame, and putting other operatives' lives in danger. For Homeland Security? No...politics, for frying out loud! Why aren't they all in jail?

And now, the **2008 Humanitarian Achievement Awards** are:

First, the **Windmills Of My Mind Award** to our local activists for marshalling the troops, making sport of the utilities, blasting us with e-mail, and fighting the electric and coal companies to push for off-shore wind power in Sussex County. You go girls...I hope that next year, when we're talking about offshore windmills we will give you the **Passing Wind Award**.

And finally, the **You Can Keep Your Head When All About Are Losing Theirs Award** to CAMP Rehoboth's Steve Elkins and Murray Archibald for being calm, mature and professional when faced with the Community Center construction delay. Although the request for the next variance had nothing to do with sex variance, Steve and Murray made sure that we remained focused and faced the issue with proper patience. In fact, this has been the hallmark of their management style as they have worked for decades, first to help build a diverse community in Rehoboth and now to help make sure our community grows and thrives. Thanks, boys and I realize the editor may want to cut this award out claiming it as too "self serving," but I am serving these awards up, fellas, not you. Thanks for all you do...and so well, too.

In closing, we want to thank our *Letters from CAMP Rehoboth* advertisers, for making these awards possible. We're out of time, so we won't do our finale – Marie Osmond singing *Fry Me to the Moon*. See you right here next year. ▼

route cheering for buff disco bunnies and topless women on motorcycles. I remember a group of women from New England what called themselves The Moving Violations. Hah! Truly, there are many facets of gaydom and it's the mix that makes us special.

We cannot marginalize the fabulous drag queens and brave bull dykes who not only wrote our history but forged our path – cajoling, prying and booting the rest of us out of the closet.

Along with our fight for the inalienable right to life, liberty, partner benefits and the pursuit of happiness, we have to protect our inalienable right to rebellion and our very own special culture. It's our tradition, part of our heritage and our roots.

So for all the progress, I still sometimes long to turn on the TV and see a grainy shot of a half-nekked gal with a Harley between her legs. I hope the networks still humor us once in awhile. ▼

OH COME ALL YE FRUITCAKES

This holiday season took the cake (that which wasn't in my mouth) for the most calorie-laden, liquor guzzling, reflux-inducing stretch of bad gustatory behavior I have ever been a party to. Or to a party. Dozens of them.

I'm not complaining. Rehoboth is such a geographically small spot and there are so many community events it's possible to enjoy several in a day.

Calculate a trio of buffets times two and a half weekend days, times four weekends in the season, and the magnitude of cookies, eggnog, red and green M&Ms, spiral hams, and Swedish meatballs I consumed is staggering. Don we now our big apparel.

In our house, the holidays started with Hanukkah Matzoh Balls and potato latkes to launch the December bloat period. Fast away the old gas passes, fa la la la la, la la la la. On Thanksgiving weekend we bought a recumbent exercise bike, vowing to start our regimen immediately to keep pace with Christmas cookies.

The first thing Bonnie did after plugging the thing into the wall was trip over it, breaking two toes. Exercise out, comfort food in.

As for me, I view exercise like drinking – not something to be done alone. Bring on the figgy pudding.

So there were cocktail parties, Wine tastings, Christmas dinners, and Harry & David goodies. See the grazing fool before us. Fa la la etc.

And of all the wretched holiday excess I subjected myself to this season, a pair of events, like my thighs, loom large.

One Sunday we enjoyed a fantastic brunch at a friend's home with Mimosas at noon, Mimosas and entrees at 3:30, and more Mimosas well into the evening. Following this alcohol marathon, I'm proud to report no hangover at all from the eight hour champagne binge. I did however have a raging case of Acid Reflux from the f-ing orange juice. It's a sad commentary about aging.

A second memorable holiday event was the Apple Pie Throw Down. Not being a Food Network foodie, I figured we were going to throw apple pie down our throats, not unlike the rest of our seasonal meals.

Turns out a Throw Down is a pie baking contest. At a party of about 25 people, four contestants took the challenge. As someone not domestically partnered with a baker, I was included among the judges.

Lobbying us, Baker and the Sous Chefs performed a cheerleading routine. A second baker noted her rich familial history among pastry chefs. Still another bragged she hadn't baked a pie in two decades (would that be humble pie?). The fourth claimed home field advantage.

All to no avail, of course, as the pies had been whisked from their makers and labeled alphabetically for a blind taste test. Wine withstanding, some judges were blinder than others.

To universal shock and awe, the winner was the person who had not had her paws in pie dough since 1988 and whose culinary repertoire consists of assembling field greens. In fact, there was suggestion of a vast right wing conspiracy, finally debunked, suggesting grocery store collaboration.

Following the pie throwing came New Year's Eve (O'er the fields we go, eating all the way) and more gluttony. Should old intentions be forgot and never brought to mind? Just how many Tums can a person take without calcifying? 10? 9? 8? 7?

Happy New Year! Let's drink a cup of Maalox please and sing of Auld Lang Syne.

Bonnie and I resolved just about the same thing everyone else in town resolved: back to sensible food and drink consumption. For yonder breaks a new and glorious morn. We hope.

And our vow was strengthened last week when were up in Philadelphia. Leaving an appointment, we stepped in front of a bank of elevators, pushed the DOWN button and waited. Soon, the wide doors opened to reveal several people already aboard. We stepped in.

As the doors closed, a booming recorded voice warned: "The elevator is now full."

Now *THAT* was humiliating.

I'll get back to the stationary bike and lean cuisine after we get back from the cruise we are about to take. Of course, that's right before Valentine's Day, followed by the Chinese New Year buffet and then the Rehoboth Chocolate Festival and let's face it, I should really have my jaw wired shut. The only Throw Down I should enter is if it's my fork.

Well, the season of excess is over. Thumpety Thump Thump o'er the bills we go.▼

February 2008

ANCHORS AWEIGH, IT'S GAY

I do not work for Olivia (the all-women travel company) and this article is not being written at the behest of Olivia Cruises. In fact, it's an article I would have bet my Schnauzers I'd never write.

And that's because I was stupid.

All these years I wrongly thought that an all-gay cruise was great for red state closeted gals and others without the freedom to live like we do here in Gayberry RFD. Fun, yes, but Olivia cruises cost more than "regular" cruises to the same ports, since Olivia is the middle-womyn. I mega-stupidly dismissed it as a luxury I didn't need.

Wrong, The Earth is flat wrong. You can't put a man on the moon wrong. George Bush wrong. *That* wrong.

So why did I go? Fifty-two Rehoboth area women were already signed up and we got a last minute half-price deal, plus a discount for an obstructed view stateroom. "Do you mind a life boat blocking your view?" asked the sales rep. "Um, let's see, the ocean this way, and 1800 women are the other way. I can see the ocean at home."

So from the minute I walked up the gangplank onto the gigunda ship docked in Ft. Lauderdale, I started learning just how criminally insane I had been.

With Men's Room signs covered with temporary letters marked Ladies, and the loudspeaker booming "Attention Women of Olivia," the party commenced.

Mandatory life boat drill, Mai Tai cocktails, unpacking. Half the ship dined early and saw kd lang in the theatre, while the other half of us saw Margaret Cho first and dined afterward. Margaret Cho was hilarious but over-the-edge filthy. I don't know whether she would have been better before or after dinner. Both headliners dazzled and outshone the one entertainment I remember from a "regular" cruise – a man playing "Oklahoma" on a saw. No kidding.

On that first night, we celebrated Olivia's 35th Anniversary with a deck party. My eyes just drank it in – young hotties, older hotties, black, white, brown, abled, disabled, thin, not thin, singles, couples, drinkers, non-drinkers and a whole lotta Rehobos. I loved the music, laughing and sights – two women dancing in wheelchairs, lovers looking out to sea, partners rocking the dance floor, singles meeting and greeting, waaay gay waiters delivering Piña Coladas, inked and pierced dyklets holding hands and middle-aged mamas stealing Anne Murray kisses in the moonlight.

I don't know what hit me, but it was like walking into a '70s gay bar for the first time or seeing a hundred thousand revelers at my first pride march. Steeped in community, feeling freer than ever, I finally experienced what it must feel like to be straight in a straight world. On the Holland American Zuiderdam, radar was gaydar and the whole damn world was the L word.

The next morning, a day at sea, sealed the deal. Comics Kate Clinton and Karen Williams hosted a film about the 35 years of Olivia – not coincidentally, the history of the entire women's movement. We laughed, cheered, met the staff, heard from entertainers Cris Williamson and Holly Near, and applauded for Col. Margarethe Cammermeyer who took on the military after they asked and she told.

Bonnie, also a long-time skeptic, hopefully clutched her door prize ticket for the two-for-one cruises they would be giving away.

There were art auctions, spa treatments, hot tubs, casino madness, singles parties, couples massage, the requisite newly-wed, oldy-wed games, rainbow trivia in the lounge, barbecues on the deck and food, food, food, drink, drink, drink.

Sometimes we dined with our posse, sometimes with folks who started out as strangers. Every elevator ride, cluster of women in a shop, or folks in rows in front or behind us at the theatre provided "Where you from? What do you do?" opportunities. Everybody smiled. Everybody had restless mouth syndrome.

While most of the fun took place on board, there were Caribbean ports.

Grand Turk is a small island with a lot of jewelry stores for tourists. But Bonnie convinced me to ride a dune buggy. I've been out of the closet over thirty years but that day I actually earned my dyke card. Bonnie (driving) and I (in my helmet and visor) took off speeding in the open frame buggy. Did I mention rain? We rode through puddles and ruts, getting splattered and speckled with clots of mud the size of chicken fingers. After two hours I looked like a Jackson Pollock canvas.

In Tortola we took a ferry to another island, Virgin Gorda, where we went swimming amid glorious boulders, caves, and rock formations. The surf was so rough (how rough was it?) that on my first foray into the ocean I got sucked up and surfed back onto the beach at 50 mph, flat on my ass. Of course, being a lesbian group, girls came shouting. "I'm a nurse! I'm a nurse, I'm a nurse!"

None needed. Even the injured pride was fun. And the water was paint chip blue.

We sampled legendary Pain Killer shots at Pusser's Saloon with a couple of young gals we met, for an evening of splendid cross-generational story swapping. Luckily, the ship's crew lined the way back to the boat, so we didn't stagger off the pier.

What would a gay cruise be without a theme night? Prior to launch our Rehoboth contingent learned of the Mad Hatter Party. Okay, we'd all need matching hats with a Rehoboth-like theme and which packed easily. One of us found perfectly silly, flat-packable fish hats. We also had matching t-shirts announcing Women of Rehoboth on the front and "what happens on the cruise, stays on the cruise" on the back. While I am telling tales here, my lips are sealed with the really juicy stuff.

Suffice it to say, that the 1746 other women on the boat took notice of the women of Rehoboth and they all now know of the fantastic gay resort on the Delaware coast. We posed for a group photo out on deck one evening and did a 54-woman strong fish-hatted conga line in the disco on Mad Hatter Night.

I hated to dock back in Florida. We had a wonderful, wonderful time. We would have gotten our money's worth at more than twice the price. Olivia is in the hospitality business and they do it well. So there. I was so very wrong.

And if you call Olivia and book a cruise, be sure to bring Visine. There's only so much eye candy you can take without back up. ▼

March 2008

I want to talk about something nobody ever talks about in public. And it's a dark, messy and dangerous place.

Get your mind out of the gutter.

I'm talking about your personal document shredder.

Right now, mine is upside down, unplugged and glaring at me with an unwanted credit card solicitation stuck in its teeth. I hate my shredder.

Remember the days when you'd get mail, read it and throw it away? So simple, so Twentieth Century.

Now that the credit pooh-bahs have convinced us that every unshredded missive is an open invitation to identity thief, I have become a slave to my shredder. I fight with it. I shriek at it. I have been known to wish it was dead. When my first shredder actually died, I had Jewish guilt.

It wasn't always this way. Back in the day, when I first took up shredding, I loved my shredder. What fun it was watching unwanted bank statements and old tax returns disappear into the maw to become confetti.

It was pretty easy, too. Three piles: file, shred, toss.

Now it's file, shred, toss, recycle. If the dollar sinks any lower it will be file, shred, toss, recycle or save for toilet paper.

How did this happen?

We heard about shredders for years, with our national security agencies using them to protect covert operations and corporate accounting firms using them to hide major fraud. Shredders let them get away with murder, both literally and figuratively.

But a shredder at home? What for?

Then came the credit police, along with cable newscasters eager to fill up that 24-hour news cycle, warning of terrifying identity theft tales. They convinced us that bypassing the shredder with a single envelope with our names, never mind an actual invoice sporting an account number, means you might as well be selling your identity on eBay.

So I got into shredding. My latest shredder (that I've owned the same number of shredders in my lifetime as I have owned coffee pots is scary) is a Professional, Heavy Duty, Cross Cut Paper Shredder with auto reverse, steel gear construction and the ability to destroy CDs and Credit Cards. I so wish I had destroyed the credit cards before I abused them.

As for the destruction of CDs, I have to admit great pleasure in trying out the machine with old Barry Manilow albums. I shred the songs the whole world sings.

But the truth is, it's tricky business this shredding. Last week I accidentally sent a CD through the paper slot and the shredder ground to a halt like a politician caught with a call girl. I spent the better part of that afternoon extracting CD shards from the shredder with a tweezers.

I'd like to calculate how many hours a week I spend shredding bank statements, credit reports, charge receipts, insurance forms and old checks. And we can't forget about all the pre-approved credit card applications with their tempting pre-approved checks.

Those damn things just beg to be stolen so some low life can charge you for a trip to Vegas. I know that what happens in Vegas stays there, but I don't want it to be my credit rating. I'm telling you, worrying about this stuff can turn you into a paranoid nut job wanting to cancel all your credit cards, close your savings accounts and start hiding your money in tomato cans in the back yard.

Remember the promise of a paperless society? This isn't it, unless we've traded an eight-and-a-half by eleven society for confetti world. And speaking of tiny speckles of paper, yesterday, I failed to put the plastic storage bucket back into the shredder properly and came home to discover two sheepish Schnauzers and a den floor that looked like a parade route after the Red Sox won the pennant.

So now I'm looking at my upended, constipated shredder,

wondering if I have to purchase yet another anti-identity theft device. By the way, my 1997 coffee pot is still brewing just fine.

I go online and read the ads for shredders. I can choose from The Shredmaster, Powershred Plus, Destroyit Heavy-Duty, Intimus (what does it shred, Hustler and condoms?), and my personal favorite, Intellishred. If it were truly intelligent it would have figured out a different way to deter dumpster divers by now. They also offer machines with child locks, which, I assume, double as Schnauzer locks.

I have learned that the average heavy-duty shredder feeds 26 - 30 sheets at a time at 30 feet per minute. I imagine that will be useful to clean up after the Bush Administration. And I loved the ad for a continuous shredding heavy duty model for non-stop shredding 24-hours a day. What kind of business needs round the clock shredding now that Enron is gone?

But here's the really frightening truth about protecting your identity and the sanctity of garbage: there has now been a documented rash of scams taking money from frightened consumers for Identity Fraud Protection.

It's probable that some of the shady characters who dove in dumpsters to steal identities in the first place may now be going door-to-door selling phony protection against such despicable acts. Unscrupulous companies are all over cyber-space selling identity theft protection for a mere $14.99 per month.

These services, with names like Trusted I.D., Privacy Protector and LifeLock (heck, I'd subscribe to Jaw Lock if they would stop sales calls at dinner time) are lurking everywhere, ready to sell us our privacy back.

Well I don't want it. Take my identity, please. I'll forward the bills.

As for replacing my shredder, the jury is still out. After all, every day I send out dozens of pieces of correspondence with name and address all over them, even as I spend time feeding the shredder with similar information.

Face it. It doesn't make a shred of sense. ▼

April 2008

I've discovered Philadelphia.

Until recently, when I thought of Philadelphia it was all about cream cheese. No longer.

I've returned from an immersion tour that included the best food experience of my life (and that's going some), watching rainbow flags go up literally and figuratively, and being asked the quintessential "Provolone or Cheese Whiz?" It doesn't get much better than that.

On the pretense that lofty topics like history and culture were tour highlights, we'll start with the Philadelphia Museum of Art. In celebration of the 100th anniversary of the artist Frida Kahlo's birth, there is a massive exhibit of her most important self-portraits and still lifes. Known for painting herself with that alarming unibrow and mustachioed upper lip, Kahlo was actually more attractive than her self-portraits – as noted in the fabulous photos from her personal albums along with the exhibit.

If you can't get there to see it in the next month or so, rent the film *Frida*, starring Salma Hayek – not only is there an unforgettable scene where Frida tangos with Ashley Judd, but you get a great look at Frida's canvasses, too.

Bonnie and I did not jog up the museum steps humming the theme from *Rocky*, but you knew that.

For history, I checked out Independence Hall. The room is tiny, with tinier windows. And July 4th, 1776 was reportedly a scorcher. Let's face it, our forefathers didn't wear cargo shorts and crocs. John Hancock and the others may have scribbled their john hancocks on the parchment just to flee the sauna.

Over at the new Constitution Center I walked among the lifesize bronzes of the document signers and a cerebral film exhibit charting our nation's quest for equality for all. I started to nurture a bad attitude, figuring that the equality quest would exclude LGBT Americans. To the curator's credit, the march toward gay equality is noted and given weight, even if there is no resolution yet. I hope I get back in my lifetime for the last reel.

For more history, I visited the old Wanamaker's Department Store which is now Macy's (isn't everything?) with its two story pipe organ and 18th century architecture. Coincidentally there was a sale and I turned history into shopping before you could say Give Me Liberty or Give me 30% off. I was, at least, using currency with Ben Franklin on it.

Later, we sampled Philly's gay culture. We did the nightlife. We got to boogie.

For the Food Tour: We started in South Philly at Jim's Steaks, family owned and operated since 1939. Sure, I've had Cheese Steaks, but I'd never been asked if I wanted Cheese Whiz on mine. According to Pennsylvania Governor Ed Rendell, it's not the real thing without the Whiz. Sorry, Guv, I couldn't go there. But the gooey provolone over steak and onions folded into a perfect roll is deservedly legend.

Going from the ridiculous to the sublime, Bonnie and I celebrated our anniversary with brunch at the Rittenhouse Hotel. Truly, I have never had a more exquisite food experience in my entire calorie-clogged, thigh-bulging, restaurant-reviewing lifetime.

We took the Rittenhouse tour-de-kitchen marathon. The buffet had over 40 appetizers alone, including oysters, caviar, vichyssoise with lobster, foie gras ganache, escargot fricassee, shrimp spatzle and the unlikely winner, pineapple and Thai basil soda.

The main course took diners into the actual kitchen for a hot buffet of every kind of meat imaginable (and some slightly unimaginable) along with seafood, paella, venison sausages, Belgian waffles, Tuscan bread pudding, Brussels sprouts and, and, and....

For dessert there was a Liquid Nitrogen station, which, I

initially thought was on loan from a dermatologist. No, the smoking stuff was for submerging coconut curry foam and dark chocolate to form divine confections.

But on to Rainbow Flags. Following the hedonistic weekend, I spoke at the National Trust for Historic Preservation Conference on the topic of "Rainbow Flags on Main Street."

I shared experiences about the economic rewards of gay-welcoming communities. We provided demographics about the value of the gay dollar (big!), and the many benefits to the community at large, not the least of which is a heightened preservation and design ethic.

I had the pleasure of explaining how CAMP Rehoboth evolved, helping to bridge the gap between gay and straight residents and business owners. Dozens of attendees wanted a how-to manual for starting their own CAMP clones. As people described small towns with fledgling gay sensibilities but no central organizing leadership, I heard CAMP-envy and realized how lucky we are.

As I was leaving the hotel to come home, dozens of city workers in bucket trucks busily installed hundreds of rainbow banners on city lampposts. The annual Equality Forum is on the horizon and the whole community will be celebrating.

The City of Philadelphia makes a great commitment to their LGBT entrepreneurs and citizens, realizing just which side their tourism toast is buttered on. In fact the City recently launched the nation's largest gay tourism marketing campaign, going after its share of the $54.1 billion gay and lesbian travel market.

Their slogan says it all: "Philadelphia: Get your history straight and your nightlife gay."

The City of Brotherly (and Sisterly) love, indeed.▼

May 2008

I never thought I'd fall in love like this again.

Gleefully giddy and blushing when I think of her, I'm in the full throes of a mad affair.

Don't phone the *National Enquirer*, Bonnie not only approves, but she introduced me to her.

I'm in love with my car – head-over-heels with my previously owned, gently-used six-year old BMW.

I swore off woman-car love in the disco era when my silver-blue 1964 Corvette convertible was hauled off on a flat bed truck, its back wheels having fallen off. We'd been together through thick (often) and thin (not so often), but the speed bump I hit that day ended it all. I'd known her most of my life.

I was there in 1964, on Lincoln's birthday (when we actually celebrated it on February 12) picking up my mother's new sports car from the dealer. It cost a whopping $4000 and everybody thought my father was nutty for buying it for his wife.

By 1968 I was permitted to drive the car to college, 250 miles from New York City to Washington, DC. Sadly, I'd learned to drive in Manhattan, meaning I could parallel park like a champ but had never driven over 30 mph. You can imagine what happened when I hit the Jersey Turnpike. By the Delaware Memorial Bridge I'd lost count of the number of middle finger salutes I'd gotten for creeping along in the right lane. It took me nine hours to get to DC and I arrived on campus shaken and needing controlled substances. Fortunately, in 1968, campus was awash with them.

I re-learned to drive in that sports car, and adored her, even as she fish-tailed away from stop signs, skidded wildly in the snow, and, in her later years, required an entire roll of Bounty Quicker-Picker-upper paper towels stuffed above the visors to keep me dry on rainy days. It was true love.

Together we campaigned, then cried, for Bobby Kennedy,

drove to the hinterlands of Wilmington, Delaware to *Hair* at the DuPont Theater and sat transfixed by the car radio as men walked on the moon. My love drove me to 1600 Pennsylvania Avenue to march against the Vietnam War, waited outside countless theatres while I rehearsed shows, honked for joy when Tricky Dick Nixon resigned, witnessed the dawn of disco and breathed her last just about the same time my heterosexuality did.

After that, my personal affairs turned happy, but I pined mightily for that car. What followed was a succession of unsatisfying relationships – a station wagon I called the Trashmobile; an old Dodge that was so broad in the beam I once ripped off the door handles on both sides getting into a parking space. Then I had some kind of American Motors contraption with no braking system whatever, which had me doing wheelies at red lights. Enter the cute little blue 1980 Chevette Bonnie drove when I met her. The very name Chevette, so near and yet so far.

By then I was out and proud, with Martina Navratilova telling me to buy a Subaru. I liked the Lesbaru. What followed was a bout of serial monogamy, as I purchased one Subaru after another, winding up with a 1998 anniversary edition Outback. We were comfortable together. Not exciting, but a marriage of convenience.

But one day that damned Subaru turned on me, blew a head gasket and left me in the lurch. For a while I made do driving Bonnie's Tracker, but it rode like a farm vehicle, skated across multiple lanes in the wind and was, to be honest, above me. So far, in fact, I had trouble climbing into the cockpit.

But Bonnie and I couldn't decide what kind of car I should get, and frankly I was not about to pay what it used to cost to buy a house, for a car that didn't send shivers up my spine. "I want my old car back," I'd whine and Bonnie knew I was talking about a 42-year-old Corvette.

One could be had, alright, but only at the cost of a new Lexus. Besides, the phrase "high maintenance girlfriend" clearly applied.

Even if I could have paid the ransom for a mid-century Corvette, the thing would have added twenty minutes to my daily commute: ten minutes to get myself down into the buckets and another ten minutes to pry myself out. Those were the days, my friend, and they were over.

Finally, one morning we stopped at a well-known luxury used car lot. My favorite salesman introduced me to a sweet little sea foam BMW convertible on the lot. One look and I heard violins. I instantly wanted to load it into a U-Haul and have it move in with me.

Surprisingly, its price tag was less than I'd pay for a new General Motors sedan and a loveless marriage.

So off we went, my Beamer and I, on our honeymoon – a drive to Broadkill Beach as I recall. Along the way I realized the two of us had some issues.

First, my garage was impenetrable. Subarus and Trackers are hardy outdoor machines, not requiring the designation "garage-kept" after their names in ads. But for the new baby, shelter was a priority. And our garage was a solid waste land-fill. I called 1-800-Got-Crap and divested ourselves of eight years of pack rat debris.

Then I determined that my love and I needed prophylactics –protection from the still overstuffed tool and book filled garage. A Beamer condom?

Bonnie and I headed downtown to find the next best thing: noodles. Not Chicken Lo Mein, but the Styrofoam noodles that keep me afloat in a swimming pool. At the store, we picked out several pink and purple perpendicular noodles and marched to the cash register. "What kinky things are you girls up to?" We just smiled.

Back home, I stapled the noodles to the pertinent book shelve edges, blunting every possible surface where a car door could connect. I gave her wide berth. Then I screwed my decorative Schnauzer plate to the front bumper and adhered the rainbow cling-on to the back.

Having spent the past two decades driving unloved and

dangerously unwashed vehicles doubling as trash cans and fast-food wrapper repositories, I'd have to change my foolish ways.

I vowed there would be no trash in my car. No eating. No coffee drinking. No scratching off scratch-offs. I would wash the car weekly and have it detailed frequently.

And I've done pretty well. I get a senior citizen discount at the car wash (my first, but I'm so cheap, I don't mind). I remove all debris from the car nightly. And as soon as my auto obsessed friend Julie tells me I need to get the dirt off my wheels, I attend to it.

I love my new car. Long may she wave. If you see me driving around, you wave too, please. ▼

May 2008

As it turns out, I'm not particularly Scrabulous. For a wordsmith, it's amazing how much I suck at playing the online version of Scrabble.

I got into this frustrating cyber game as a consequence of my foray into the baffling and relentless world of social networking. And it seems to be taking over my life. Social networking is like an online social disease. I don't know how I got it and it won't go away.

It started when I got an e-mail invitation from a friend to join Facebook. You know me, I hate turning down invitations. Once I joined, I was instructed to ask all my friends to join as well. After days of adding myself as a friend to folks with Facebook pages and then inviting old and new friends to my own fledgling Facebook page, things started to spin out of control.

I began hearing from people from the great beyond – like back in college or even high school, plus I was getting invitations to become friends with people I didn't even remember. It was the invitations to become friends with friends of friends that started making me crazy. I was so busy inviting friends to join Facebook and then My Space, I got confused and started inviting people to join My Face.

And was that face red when buddies asked me what Facebook was all about and I had no bloody idea.

The next thing I knew, I received cyber Petunias from a site called Green Patch and was invited to send people cyber shrubbery to help raise money to save the rain forest. I tried to figure out how to forward flowers to a bunch of folks but at the end of the day I got so flustered I'm probably responsible for the loss of several hundred acres along the Amazon.

And speaking of Amazon, there's a Facebook thing called Bookshelf, which somebody invited me to join. For the next several days I used every waking moment clicking on books I've read and writing mini-reviews of them so the Bookshelf geeks – whoever they are – will understand my reading preferences to recommend books for me. I checked off everything from *Catcher in the Rye* to *Kite Runner*. At one point, in the upper right hand portion of my screen appeared the words YOU ARE NOT READING ANYTHING RIGHT NOW. Of course not, you cyber poops, I'm filling up my virtual bookshelf and wasting time writing book reports when I could have been doing something productive like playing online Scrabble.

It's bad enough when you put your hand in the Scrabble bag and pull out all vowels in a regular game, but when the computer sticks you with iiieeoa who do you bitch at? One afternoon the dogs found me screaming at my flat screen monitor and wondered if it had peed in the house.

Meanwhile back at Facebook, friends and acquaintances are inviting me to join all kinds of communities, like college alumni associations, sports team groups, The National Sarcasm Society. That one was a temptation. And I just got invited to spend time answering movie quizzes and writing movie reviews. This will be a great way to fill my time when I'm in the rest home, but right now there's stuff happening in the real world and I'm sitting here writing a review of *Spaceballs*. Somebody help me.

Best I can tell, cyber social networking is a self-fulfilling prophecy because if you do it right you have no time for real life social networking.

I finally located the "cancel" link for the movie quiz thing and so far I have confined myself to joining just four Facebook groups – Saints & Sinners Authors (writers who participate annually in a New Orleans LGBT literary conference), One Million Strong for Marriage Equality (it can't hurt), and Six Gay Degrees of Separation, which is a group trying to get one million gay people to sign up so it can make use of our cyber muscle to fight for our rights.

And in the middle of all this social networking somebody

poked me. It didn't hurt, but I had no idea why I'd been poked.

Apparently poking is the online equivalent of somebody sticking their index finger in your shoulder. I hate that for real, so getting poked online is especially insulting. On the other hand, cyber hugging, another Facebook activity, is less irritating but no more satisfying. Hugging should be a contact sport, dontcha think?

Then there's the wall thing, where your online friends can leave you messages. I haven't written on the walls since I was five years old. Okay you boomers, remember the TV show Crusader Rabbit where you got a plastic thing to put on the TV screen and you could trace the rabbit's whereabouts? One day, with my burnt umber crayon I wrote right off the screen, onto the floor and up the wall. The parents were not amused.

But now, in my dotage, I'm being asked to write on people's walls. If texting is the new phone call, writing on somebody's wall is the new e-mail. Every day I get messages from friends who have written on my wall.

Naturally, I feel compelled to write back, since everybody can see your site and see who wrote on your wall and see the time when they wrote it and know if you have been prompt in answering or, instead, you are blowing people off in favor of your online Scrabulous game. The pressure to be responsive and clever is positively crushing.

Then there's the "Fay is…" at the top of my Facebook page. You're supposed to write what you are doing at the moment, but nobody writes "Answering this question on Facebook," which is what they are all doing, because like me they are hooked on this idiotic social networking site. I can't even write that I'm playing online Scrabble because I had to forfeit my turn because I had all vowels again.

Frankly, I can't be doing anything else, like reading the paper, doing the laundry or finishing my column, because these Facebook questions are requiring so much of my time. So once again I answer "Fay is…trying to keep up with Facebook…."

Oops, it's my turn in Scrabulous. I get a whopping three points for the word "ass." Yes indeedy.

Your move. And make it snappy. I've got to go write on several people's walls, recommend some books, fill out a questionnaire about my taste in music, and see who else is friends with all my friends so I can add more friends and write on more walls and recommend more movies and....

Somebody poke me in the eye and get me off this Facebook page. My column is due by midnight tonight and I still haven't started.

"Fay is...panicking." Somebody help her. ▼

Dorothy Allison, author of the astonishing and brilliant *Bastard Out of Carolina* who was taking my side in the debate.

Wow. For a minute I was too humbled to speak again.

I got over it.

Pretty soon talk shifted to Augusten Burroughs whose five memoirs and essay collections have been *New York Times* best sellers. His memoir *Running With Scissors* was positively heart-breaking and hilarious all at once, but its veracity has been challenged in the courts. The loony (according to the author) psychiatrist that Burroughs went to live with after his mother abandoned him – the shrink who purportedly predicted good or bad days by the positions of his turds in the toilet – sued the author for defamation and falsehoods and the case was settled out of court. When I thought the memoir was all true, I was much less disgusted by the telltale turd story.

In the final analysis, everyone on the panel and in the audience that day pretty much agreed. Truth matters. The controversy is in the degrees. And I guess that's what makes horse races and good memoir.

It's a pity Scott McClellan's book about the Bush adminis-tration hadn't come out yet. The former press secretary's scathing indictment of his White House days has members of the Bush team shrieking "Liar, liar, pants on fire!" Somehow, I am certain that McClellan subscribes to the Dorothy Allison theory of memoir – shirts, shoes and truth required.

Meanwhile, back at the conference, we all partied together – and how it gets retold in memoir will surely be very different for each of us.

In my case I was thrilled to be sharing stories and cocktails with Dorothy Allison, mystery writer JM Redman, and the many friends I have made over the years in New Orleans. When I get around to writing about the adventure I will not leave out the part about my spouse sleeping it off in the bathtub, yours truly knocking over more than one Hurricane at the Good Friends bar or hanging out with our boyfriends at a tavern where scantily clad boys cavorted on the bar. And you can bet your sweet Hurricane, I may change the names to protect the guilty and leave out a boring incident or two, but the gist of the tale will be: we were fried and it was true.

Memoirs are made of these.▼

APOCALYPSE IN 2012?

The headline on my computer screen said "Thousands expect apocalypse in 2012." That's right, according to various survival groups, and based on a millennium-old Mayan ritual, the world will be kaput in less that four years – specifically on December 21, 2012. I hope Hanukah comes early that December so I get my presents.

And frankly, if my political party doesn't take over the White House come November I tend to agree with the timetable.

Listen to this: in 2006, a book called *2012: The Return of Quetzalcoatl* was published and has sold thousands of copies a month. That beats *As I Lay Frying* on Amazon by, well, thousands of copies a month. And while authors disagree about what the heck to expect on that day in December I'm sure we will be easy prey as we all sit around trying to pronounce Quetzalcoatl.

Gee, if the schedule holds, no retirement for me. I just turned 60 and I'm officially in the first wave of 78 million baby boomers – a huge demographic bulge (not me, personally, but there are days…) that will, hopefully, age better than our parents and grandparents did. At least we hope we will.

In fact, not to be mistaken for a fuddy-duddy, I partied on my recent birthday like I was 30. The sad truth hit when I woke up the next day feeling every bit of 90. From what I understand, I was led out of my favorite watering hole and deposited into a taxi. My own personal Armageddon. Why wait for 2012?

And, although it happened five days later, I considered it a belated gift when Senator Jesse Helms passed. On the same day fireworks went off in Rehoboth. Coincidence?

When I wasn't reading about the end of the world, I was enjoying my birthday cards. Like the one that said "Anything Worth Doing is Worth Over-doing." See Armageddon paragraph above.

Forget about *Last Comic Standing* – I think the most hilarious comedians are now at Hallmark. For example, "What do older women have between their breasts that younger women don't?"

"A belly-button."

Birthday cards have gone hi-tech. Knowing my youthful indiscretion of marrying an accordion player, my friends delight in watching me twitch and squirm at accordion humor. This year I got a musical card featuring a song on the wretched instrument.

I loved the talking card. On the front was written "I was looking through cards trying to find one for your birthday and I was laughing so hard I ..."

You open the card and hear "Clean up on aisle 6...." Ah, Depends humor.

I have to admit, though, a disturbing thing did happen on my birthday. I found myself driving in the middle lane on Route One with my left blinker on for no apparent reason. I knew I'd eventually become a doddering old fart but I didn't think it would happen this fast.

But there seems to be good news on the horizon. Today, on CBS News online, another article on the aging of baby boomers, or in my case gayby boomers reported "...signs suggest...that boomers will enjoy not just increased longevity but better health as well. Boomers may be aging more slowly than previous generations because of healthy habits, such as less smoking and more exercise. Maybe 60 really *is* the new 50."

Gee, I hope so. But that brings me to the next question. If we are going to live longer lives, how are we going to pay for them?

If I positively knew that the Mayan doomsday was coming, Mamma Mia could I have a great four years. Bring on the wine, women, song and Hostess Ho-Hos. But Quetzalcoatl, even if you could pronounce it, might not happen, and in that case, I have to figure out how long my money is going to last.

Perhaps as a result of this big birthday, or the fact that I'd for the operation. My mate is a vet and due to our nation's health care crisis, the VA is her only health insurance option. Thank God for that safety net. But…there are issues.

Bonnie was already hooked up to the IV, wearing the little surgical hat, and surrounded by a flock of medical personnel, and we were on hold – both in the OR and on the phone with the VA.

"Just go over there and get what they need, Fay," the patient said. "It's only a few blocks away."

"Wait," said a nurse. "You better take your documents, and maybe we should sign something telling them you're allowed to get the information. You know the HIPPA privacy rules."

"Oh, right, we're not legally married. Crap." Whereupon no less than six doctors and nurses, all held up by the snafu, scribbled on a note pleading for me to be considered worthy of the patient information.

With a giant plastic bag filled with Bonnie's clothes and our voluminous legal dossier slung over my shoulder, I raced to the lobby and hopped a cab to the VA hospital. I will spare you the details, but I was shuttled around to three offices and on hold with several non-compliant people as I frantically pictured a gaggle of expensive health care workers loitering by Bonnie's gurney. At one point I was on hold from the lobby to the business office, listening to an educational tape about the seven signs of a heart attack and I was having eight of them.

Finally somebody agreed to call Bonnie's surgeon and set things right. Heart pounding, I ran back downstairs and saw a shuttle bus. "Does that go by Penn Presbyterian?" I asked.

"Yep. It's for the vets. Are you a vet?"

"I'm the spouse of a vet."

"What's his name?"

"It's a her." Shit. What was I thinking? Toto, we're NOT in Rehoboth.

"Then you can't be no spouse."

Bet me. I may or may not have said a very bad word, swung my big plastic trash sack over my shoulder and, channeling Lily Tomlin's bag lady, marched out the door and huffed and puffed uphill six blocks to return to the operatory.

Amazingly, the surgery finally happened a scant seven hours late, all went well and we headed home the next day.

Just let me say this about the past week. There's a reason I work in public relations, not health care. I tried to be a good nurse, really I did, but it just isn't in my skill set.

Bonnie came home with a 36-inch leg brace to prevent knee bends and the thing is held together with a thousand strips of industrial strength Velcro. You have to be the Incredible Hulk to unstick it (which, I might become after spending a week as Clara Barton) and when you do get the Velcro open it instantly sticks to everything in the vicinity.

I've spent whole days peeling it off rugs, furniture, and pajamas. One time Moxie got up in Bonnie's recliner when the thing was undone and we thought she'd be spending the next few weeks dragging a schnauzer around by his beard. I stepped on a Velcro strip in my socks and took the appliance with me like toilet paper on a shoe.

Then there was the dressing to change and the blood thinning injections, not to mention the matzoh ball soup to prepare. I don't know whether this house was more like *House*, *ER* or *Nip/Tuck* (me taking a nip of Grey Goose after tucking the patient into bed), but somehow we did all right.

I survived the nursing rotation, Bonnie started getting back on her feet, and no schnauzers were injured in the making of this column. Well, except for a little fur flying when we snipped it off the Velcro from hell.

But in our hibernation, as we watched the evening news and its giddy coverage of same-sex couples tying the knot on the West Coast, I unpacked our thick file of papers notarizing our coupledom. And I still had the scribbled emergency letter to the VA, signed by Dr. Kildare and his entire surgical team.

Hell, according to the front desk guy at the VA, for my civil rights I didn't have to go to the back of the bus, I couldn't even get on the bus. Which tells me we have a long way to go.

Code Blue, voters. And stat.▼

August 2008

Lots of people, most recently gay conservative (oy, an oxymoron) Andrew Sullivan, have been speculating about the death of gay culture.

I say, not so fast.

Yes, it's true, as Sullivan reports about Provincetown, "No one bats an eye if two men walk down the street holding hands, or if a lesbian couple pecks each other on the cheek, or if a drag queen dressed as Cher careens down the main strip on a motor scooter...."

It could be Rehoboth.

So too, like in Rehoboth, does Sullivan report that the "real-estate boom has made Provincetown far more expensive than it ever was, slowly excluding poorer and younger visitors and residents...beautiful, renovated houses are slowly outnumbering beach shacks...the number of children of gay couples has soared...bar life is not nearly as central to socializing as it once was. Men and women gather on the beach, drink coffee on the front porch of a store, or meet at the Film Festival."

It could certainly be Rehoboth. It's also true that our separate and formerly underground gay culture did develop, in most part, to combat, mask and soothe the twentieth century attacks against us.

That being said, the vicious attack part may not be so evident anymore in Provincetown or Rehoboth, but how about Oklahoma? I saw a lunatic Oklahoma County Commissioner candidate on TV showing off his official campaign mailing piece – a homophobic comic book showing gays as pedophiles (spelled wrong in the piece by the way) and Satan affiliated with his opponent's campaign. The candidate defended his despicable homophobia with the calm righteousness of a defender of tax policy.

Also this week I heard about the latest Bush administration

boondoggle. They have instructed the tabulators for the 2010 census to take the forms of couples who self-identify as being in gay marriages and *change* them to read "unmarried partners." That includes legal gay marriages from California and Massachusetts. I don't know about you, but I will not be erased.

But it was last week, at the Blue Moon Restaurant, when I realized our gay culture will be everlasting. I was there, a lone lesbian in a sea of guys (further cementing my odd reputation as an honorary gay man) to see comic actor Leslie Jordan do his hilarious and amazingly poignant one man show.

I knew that folks of my generation related to Jordan's tales of surviving youth as an effeminate young man and transition-ing from suffocating shame to celebratory pride – but I was surprised that so many younger men in the crowd laughed so easily and applauded so enthusiastically with recognition.

Jordan himself, noting his work with The Trevor Project in L.A., referred to our continuing need to have safe places for teens and young adults who are being attacked, shunned or in despair because society has told them to be ashamed of themselves.

Heck, it's not just young people. All over the country, even here in Sussex County, some gay men and women expect less of their lives and less of themselves because they have been instilled with shame and internal homophobia.

As long as youngsters are still being ostracized because they are presumed gay, and as long as teens are attacked, physically or emotionally for being gay, and as long as jobs and lives are at stake unless gays remain closeted, there will be a need for gay culture – a safe family, a safe place to be and a special culture of our own.

This is why CAMP Rehoboth is so important to our community. Sure, some of us, in our, ahem, maturity are less inclined to stay up to the wee hours dancing at the July 4th LOVE Dance. We may not need the library of LGBT books or spend quite as much time as we did in the courtyard, but whether we know if or not, we still need it. Whether people who have NEVER participated in a CAMP event know it or not, they benefit from CAMP's existence, too.

CAMP is the reason we can be comfortable in this town and its vigilance is the reason Rehoboth will continue to welcome all kinds of families. CAMP's police sensitivity training helps our summer officers be more comfortable interacting with our community; CAMP's support of the women's golf league has helped more than one golfer tell me that joining the league made her feel part of the community; CAMP's advocacy for LGBT citizens is the reason local and state governments respect us as a constituency; the welcoming atmosphere created by CAMP has helped a variety of religious organizations, non-profits and clubs open their doors to the gay community. Oh, and CAMP's successful publication has gays and non-gays alike advertising and reading.

Speaking of diversity, our favorite female impersonator, Christopher Peterson, in his show has an audience also made up of gays and non-gays. But everyone is enjoying our culture, our icons, our stereotypes, and our jokes on our terms.

This weekend, at the Convention Center, we will enjoy the CAMP Follies, celebrating our culture. We will be poking fun at headlines that affect us, incidents that make us mad, politicians who hate us, and more. And it's our culture to satirize.

Yes, it would be great to think that some day being gay will be a non-issue. But if that day ever comes, our glorious gay culture will remain alive and well. We may not need it for protection anymore, but the fact remains that we're here, we're queer and we understand each other. Our gay culture is not what makes us queer, but it's what makes us queers smile.

We will not be erased and we will not erase our gay culture. Count on it. ▼

August 2008

I just got back from Phoenix, Arizona where it was 114 degrees at high noon. Everybody told us we'd be okay, it was dry heat. Please. You could fry a frittata on the bench in front of the hotel. I got third degree burns of the frittata.

This was some fancy schmancy resort, with rooms going for $500 dollars a night in the season. That would be winter. In August, they say "Let the lesbians have it for a literary conference." It's practically free for a fabulous room, impeccable service and, when you go outside, you feel like you're hiking inside a blow dryer.

The conference – Golden Crown Literary Society – celebrated lesbian writers and books published in 2007. And it was wonderful. I was invited to speak on the topic of humor, which historically, lesbians as a species are thought to lack. I started class with the old joke "How many lesbians does it take to change a light bulb?" Answer: "That's not funny." Fortunately, the crowd tittered.

Afterwards, at the gorgeous pool, we dunked in the cool water. We got out to eat lunch but two bites into the meal we dizzied from the heat and settled for sucking frozen Margaritas through a straw while applying the frosty glass to our wrists.

Two minutes later, lest heat stroke set in, we violated the sacrosanct parents' rule and did not wait the requisite half hour after eating before swimming. For the record, we did not get the oft-threatened cramps, but I nearly needed a tour of the local burn unit after touching the metal pool ladder. Three minutes after that we were back inside the hotel.

At 6 p.m. (109 degrees) some sadist suggested a visit to the Wild West Tourist town on hotel property. We survived the four minute walk across the steaming desert parking lot, entered "town," and immediately got "caught" in a faux gun fight.

Three suspected out of work actors, poor bastards, "killed" each other, winding up flayed out in the desert dirt.

Hoping heat exhaustion didn't lay me out next, we set off for the saloon, by way of the air-conditioned "jail." The "sheriff" offered shotgun wedding re-enactments for a fee. We decided not to ask for a same-sex shotgun wedding, unclear whether they had access to live ammunition.

Finally, we guzzled a beer and got the hell out of Dodge, thrilled to be heading for A/C and being able to use the phrase "got the hell out of Dodge" literally. At the hotel, where it was now a balmy 106 degrees, I studied the architecture and wondered if the three-sided adobe/concrete entrance was supposed to replicate a Pee Posh Indian pueblo oven. See the Mesquite grilled columnist stagger into the lobby.

At the Saturday night award ceremony and reception, we met and talked to readers and writers from all over the country. A reader of my books marched up to Bonnie and said "Gee, I'd pictured you as much more butch." Neither of us knew what to do with that comment, so Bonnie just smiled, butchly.

Conference organizers had arranged for two Native American men to entertain us before the awards. Following applause for the intricate dance, one performer told us he was an attorney, working on Native American human rights issues and likened their fight against discrimination to that of the gay women in the room. In the early 1900s the Gila River had been diverted by non-natives, causing entire communities to disappear from lack of water. Recently, a series of dams helped reverse that action, so the Maricopa tribe has its water back, along with mammoth casinos, sucking dollars from the white man, which is eminently fair.

On Sunday, we left the hotel for a drive in our air-conditioned rental car up Superstition Mountain – a collection of hills, mesas, buttes, and cacti I had previously only seen in TV westerns. I expected black and white. But no, it was all in living brown. A sign at a scenic pull-off warned us not to put our hands anywhere where we couldn't see them. As if I ever would.

The rutted dirt road wound up the mountainside, with nary a guard rail and two way traffic comin' round the mountain, hauling boats, campers, and head-ons waiting to happen. Neither of us fears heights, but it was a hair-raising ride, worthwhile for the awesome canyon, gully and mountain views. We were warned to beware of wildlife, and although we kept a wary lookout, the wildest life we saw were several Geico spokesnewts running across the road. We did see the rare and gorgeous blooming cactus flowers – rare because only a handful of morons are stupid enough to visit the desert in August to see them.

Next, we visited a friend of Bonnie's who lives in a terrific resort and retirement community for lesbians called The Pueblo in Apache Junction, AZ. Hundreds of women live there, only the place was nearly deserted because it was August and these lesbians have the good sense to go north for the summer. Like Care Free resort in Florida, Rainbow Vision in Santa Fe and potentially one eventually here in Sussex County, more and more of these retirement options are springing up. Who'd a thunk it back before Stonewall.

Our final weekend adventure was getting home. Let's face it, air travel sucks these days. Between the complimentary CAT scan, an over-sold plane in Phoenix, and thunder storms closing runways in Atlanta, it actually took us a half hour longer to get from Phoenix to Philly than it did to get home from Beijing.

In hindsight, for scenic views and lesbian literature it was a wonderful trip. And I learned a few things.

1. Pricey resorts can count on us cheap lesbians to save their asses off-season.

2. When it's too hot to eat you do not save calories by drinking frozen cocktails.

3. I newly respect the term "You're toast."

4. And when people say "It's not the heat, it's the humidity," tell them they are full of crap.

Back in Rehoboth, the thermometer said 92 degrees. Felt like a cold snap. ▼

DON'T HASSLE ME, I'M LOCAL

Can I bitch?

I was driving on Rehoboth Avenue yesterday when the car in front of me screeched to a stop, punched his flashers and sat behind a car with its trunk flung open. Clearly a visitor. Now you and I, but obviously not the fellow in the double parked car, know that an open trunk is a sign of, well, an open trunk. And it often bears no relation to whether people are packing up to leave the parking space.

So the light is green, but nobody can go because this yutz is waiting in case a space opens up this millennium. Finally, after stowing strollers that look like steam rollers, kites, boogey boards, coolers and a little league team, car number one tries to pull out, but car number two is camped behind it with nowhere to go because cars me through ten are gridlocked. Amid the sonata for horns, everybody misses their dinner reservation. Sometimes I wonder if vacationers leave their brains and manners back home with the cat.

I love the Saturday Night Fights. People drive around, see a vacant parking space and drop off the frailest person in the car to stand in the spot until the vehicle can come back around the block to claim it. Naturally, in the interim, six football players in a steroid rage drive up in a Humvee, leaving grandma to defend her position. Trust me, chivalry is as dead as Richard Nixon.

I actually witnessed somebody almost run over a tween saving a spot for Daddy's Caddy. It's like Armegeddon out there, with Category 6 screaming matches. Mind you, these are the same people who jog up and down the boardwalk and run 10ks. God forbid they'd have to walk a block and a half to buy taffy.

Our traffic circle on the way in and out of town is another crime scene. The circle actually works pretty well for anybody who reads the sign "Yield to traffic in circle." What part of IN CIRCLE don't they understand?

Cars race to the circle and play chicken with drivers coming around from their left, practically playing bumper cars. If drivers entering the circle do yield, they often don't know when to come out of their coma. Here's a tip. If there's room for two Budweiser trucks and a team of Clydesdales between you and the car coming around the circle, move your ass.

Conversely, some fool is IN the circle but sees a car approaching and stops to let it in. Like lemmings, every car downtown now floods the circle and the goofball who stopped can cancel his hotel reservation because he'll still be sitting there by morning. Chivalry is as dead as Herbert Hoover.

Of course, our visiting pedestrians can disrupt traffic brilliantly as well. Throngs of aggressive jaywalkers, pushing fleets of baby strollers leap into the streets whenever they feel like it, making the screech of tires as ubiquitous a summer sound as chirping sea gulls. Yesterday I saw a man holding a pizza box with the lid up, eating a slice as he tried to cross the road. Do you want a seeing eye dog with that pepperoni?

And what's with the befuddled curb huggers, forgetting that green means go and red means stay. Nightly, they do the "should I stay or should I go?" dance on the corner, with their choice bearing no relation to traffic signals. It's like whack-a-mole in the street, only nobody gets a stuffed bear.

Down here on the sand, behavior is even worse. I see people arriving in moving vans, setting up the Kennedy compound, with pop-up shelters, portable gazebos (with mesh ventilating panels) beach cabanas, collapsible tables and industrial sized coolers. I love the ad for the cabana with a zippered door, offering "to keep out the sun and the sand." If I wanted to keep out the sun and sand I'd be on a bar stool on Baltimore Avenue.

And then these homesteaders plop their village directly in front of me, not five feet from my chair. Seriously, people 15-feet of sand is the demilitarized zone.

Have you seen the new 8-foot umbrellas that could shelter half of Haiti? One good gust and the things will be in Portugal. Oh, that's right, they come with anvils on the bottom to anchor them. And don't forget the wireless laptop and video games. It's the beach, people, bring a towel, a hat and a book (preferably, mine).

And these same imbeciles have no concept that at some point, given that the moon revolves around the earth, the tide will come in. They always look so shocked and expect us to move back, or worse, welcome them into our family. Am I rude not to want strangers' butts scooting onto my towel?

And what's with those footballs that make noise? Tossing a pig skin I can understand, but one that whistles Dixie is just annoying.

And while time flies when you are having fun, sand flies when your kids run in flip flops around my head. Leaving the beach? Check which way the wind is blowing. I know you want to shake out your towel, but I don't need a complimentary dermabrasion. Well, maybe I do but that should be my decision.

Look, I want you to enjoy your rock music, but stick it in your ear. Personally, I'd rather hear show tunes but you wouldn't want me to subject your posse to *Hello, Dolly*, would you? And of course, do not feed the sea gulls. When you go home we're left with gulls dive bombing us like we were Tippi Hedren in *The Birds*.

And finally, the reason dogs are not allowed on our board-walk anymore (they are allowed in areas of the beach at the state park and for that I am grateful), is directly related to the visitor behavior I witnessed yesterday. A lady pulls into a parking spot, gets out with her small fluffy poodle, sees the No Dogs on Boardwalk sign, picks up the pooch and sashays onto the boardwalk anyway. A police officer sees her, and she says "I'll just hold her." He tries to be nice, smiles and looks the other way.

Then the woman puts Fifi down to make a Great Dane-sized deposit on the boardwalk. And leaves! Chivalry is as dead as Rin Tin Tin.

Okay, I know my town owes a world of gratitude to our wonderful visitors, but look, it's 104 degrees out and I'm grumpy. I will now drag my little beach chair down to the water and try to cool off. Ahhhhhhh. There, there, I'm better now. Thanks for indulging me. And come visit. I know you'll behave.▼

September 2008

I'M HERE, I'M QUEER, I'M TALKING ABOUT IT

There was a breathtaking array of lesbiana at the state park beach last weekend. The sand and parking lot overflowed with so many dykes (and their gayboy friends and canine companions) that at one point rangers posted a temporary moratorium – cars bursting with lesbians had to wait to get into the parking lot until other vehicles filled with happy galpals left. That's a lot of women. I hear there were schools of dolphins jumping up to watch the lesbians.

As for me, I was plopped on the sand in the midst of it all, admiring the scenery. After all, as a similarly married friend reported, "Just because I'm on a diet doesn't mean I can't read the menu."

Later, at Poodle Beach, at the south end of our boardwalk, thousands and thousands of gay men (and not a few women) staked out compounds on the sand to watch the annual Drag Volleyball game.

"Did you ever see so many good looking men in one place in your life?" I asked a straight friend on hand for the festivities.

"It's incredible," she said, slightly glazed over and suffering from the water, water, everywhere and not a drop to drink syndrome. "It's a whole world I know nothing about."

She was right. I'm so steeped in our history and culture I forget millions of people have no idea they know any gay people, much less about our lives. And of course, those are the champion gay-haters.

Do you know the infamous story about late Supreme Court Justice Powell, who, after casting his landmark vote against Hardwick in the pivotal Georgia sodomy case, and handing the gay equality movement a thumping setback, said to his trusted aide "actually, I don't believe I've ever met a homosexual." Of course, the aide was a great big closet queen.

The corollary is the legendary tale about General

Eisenhower who, in the early 1940s was about to issue an order rounding up all lesbians in the army and discharging them. "Well, you'd better start with me," said his long-time secretary, handing Ike a big surprise and leading to cancellation of the orders.

Yeah, that was ages ago, but despite our current visibility it sometimes surprises me how unfamiliar some people are with our lives.

Which is why, as Oct. 11 Coming Out Day approaches every year I try to share my culture where I can. This year, a chance fell in my lap when an office acquaintance asked me to go for a cup of coffee. As she nervously started to babble, I knew we weren't talking tourism.

Sure enough, she soon let loose, panicky tears dripping down her face, reporting that her son told her he was gay. The guy's a New York actor and airline steward. How didn't she know? But then it proves my point.

"And I'm so sad because of the hard life he's going to have," she said.

Oh boy. Where to start?

I began by suggesting that his coming out was the beginning of the *end* of his hard life.

"But what kind of life can it be, without a family, with the whole world hating him?"

Wow. I forget that people who don't know same-sex families with kids, don't have gay or transgender friends or relatives, or have no idea Liza Minnelli married two gay men, still exist. Worse, if they think about us at all, figure we come from Pluto.

Jeesh. Homo 101, here I go.

Through two Venti lattes I babbled about positive things she didn't know about the gay community and, set her – if you'll excuse the expression – straight about some things she thought she did know. I dropped so many names it was like the homo version of Billy Joel's "Start the Fire." When I mentioned Merv Griffin, her mouth fell open. And somewhere between Elton

John and Eleanor Roosevelt I finally said, "Look, just let me tell you about my exotic weekend and scandalous gay life."

"This weekend my partner and I went to a catered 25th anniversary party ("You're kidding. 25 years?"), went to a benefit auction ("Two women bid HOW MUCH for a cruise?"), frequented a restaurant where people don't go into anaphylactic shock if we have a romantic dinner, and ended up on the boardwalk, watching the full moon reflect in the ocean and pigging out on beach fries and custard."

She: "Well that's not a gay thing"

Me: "Exactly".

Okay, I admit it. I left some of the more colorful tales of Drag Volleyball for her post-graduate class.

But I think she felt a lot more hopeful about her son's future. Frankly, it sounds to me like he's having a blast.

Which is why I'm more convinced than ever we should live our lives in the sunshine. We're here, we're queer, let's talk about it. We should make an extra effort to be visible and share our culture. People really need to know they know happy homosexuals.

And frankly, I think Liza needs a girlfriend.▼

September 2008

Gusts of wind have certainly been howling at the beach and on television.

With the line of hurricanes blowing by and the string of partisans blowing smoke on the tube it's been quite a few weeks.

Of course, my favorite storm was Hurricane Fay, spelled correctly at that. Bonnie and I had a glorious time listening to all the reports (Fay is intensifying; Fay is boomeranging; Fay is heading for Guantanamo!) but as the saying goes, it's all fun and games until somebody gets hurt. I was gearing up to have great fun at Hurricane Fay's expense, not to mention columnist Fay's expense when I heard that the storm had killed a lot of people. Ditto for Gustav, Hannah and Ike. Suddenly it's not such fun anymore.

Which is just as well since there are sooo many other things to focus on from the past few weeks.

Speaking of forces of nature, I have to mention the passing of Del Martin, one of the true pioneers of lesbian rights. She and her partner of 55 years, Phyllis Lyons, started the very first lesbian rights organization in this country, the Daughters of Bilitis – named for a fictional friend of Sappho. As a couple, Del and Phyllis reminded me so much of my friends Anyda and Muriel, also together over half a century before they both died in 2006. I have to laugh, because Muriel always said that the term Bilitis sounded like a terrible disease and she wanted no part of it.

Together, Del and Phyllis wrote the book *Lesbian/Woman* published in 1972. I remember lurking in the dark, outside the Lambda Rising Bookstore in Washington, D.C. in 1978, screwing up my courage to go inside and buy the book. While the picture of 1972 lesbian life wasn't pretty – women's softball, seedy bars in bad neighborhoods and butch/femme partnerships, Del and Phyllis were the first to tell me that long-term lesbian relationships did actually exist and that a satisfying life might be possible – even without playing softball, god forbid.

The sadness of Del's passing was assuaged a little knowing that she and Phyllis were invited to be the first legal gay union in California. A photo of the 80-somethings cutting their wedding cake looked gorgeous on the front pages of newspapers across the country. In a statement after Del died, Phyllis Lyons said, "I am devastated, but I take some solace in knowing we were able to enjoy the ultimate rite of love and commitment before she passed." Amen.

The political conventions were forces of nature on their own. I almost lost my mind listening to pundits babbling about the speeches, even stooping to babble during the speeches. I was forced to turn to CSPAN just to get some peace and quiet.

Leaving the subjects of the economy, universal health care, the economy, the Iraq mess and the economy aside, let me just focus on the potential for gay and lesbian equality, relative to the two parties.

Um, Barack and Joe are our friends. They want to get rid of that stupid "Don't Ask, Don't Tell," favor making it illegal to discriminate against us in housing and jobs, and actually believe we should be treated equally – including making certain we have the same rights as married couples whatever the convoluted language turns out to be.

With the dismissive back of the hand, McCain and especially Palin are against civil unions and equal rights, and think discrimination against gays in jobs and housing is just fine. Not to wish Cindy or Mr. Hockey Mom any harm, but I wonder if John or Sarah will ever have to sit, crying, in the emergency room and, considered to be scum, kept from visiting their critically ill loved one? Just asking.

And how about Hillary? What part of the line "Were you voting for me or what I stand for?" don't the gay women threatening to vote for Sarah Palin understand?

In the annals of "cutting off your nose to spite your face," this is a doozy. Let's elect a woman who doesn't want women to have a choice regarding reproduction even if it's rape or incest; a woman who voted to take back partner benefits from Alaskans; a women who wanted to ban books from the library; a women who supports "Don't Ask"; a woman who wants to teach creationism in public schools and a woman who, despite compelling evidence to the contrary, thinks Abstinence Education works. Good God, it's Phyllis Schlafly in mukluks.

One bright spot can now be found weeknights at 9 p.m. on MSNBC. Rachel Maddow, an incredibly bright, insanely clever, terribly attractive young lesbian now has her own left-leaning TV news and commentary show. I know she will be preaching to the choir, but watching her makes me smile, cheer and realize I am not alone in my views. In fact, I finally understand why a brigade of dittoheads loves to listen to Limbaugh. Well, at least this is one for my side.

Meanwhile, do you want the person who is a heartbeat from the presidency to be someone whose top credential is field dressing a moose? Did I say that with my outside voice???

I'm done now. Maybe the meteorologists were right when they described Hurricane Fay as a wide swath of gusting wind. Sorry if I've offended. But this election, not only is it the economy, stupid, it's all the rest of the issues. And I hope people vote based on them, whatever their choice.

My name is Fay Jacobs and I approved this column. ▼

ONLY AS OLD AS YOU FEEL???

I'm going to get the senior ticket price at the film festival this year and I have decidedly mixed emotions about it. Sure, saving a buck sounds good, but the implications of accepting the discount are horrifying.

Turning 60 hit me like a ton of Metamucil.

So I decided to monitor my behavior to determine if I was merely mathematically challenged or if I was actually a bonafide old fart.

You be the judge.

At a recent 20th anniversary party, revelers of a certain age crammed the dance floor for the disco tunes, hands waving over our heads for "Gloria," while the stomping and clapping for "We Are Fam-i-ly" shook the party tent. Nice and spry.

Later, as dozens of women headed to their cars, I heard somebody whisper "sciatica," and another cop to a frozen shoulder. Feeling youngish, Bonnie and I only let out a few small wheezes.

The next day at a golf league party, about a hundred women rocked to the music and sang along with ABBA. I have to admit to drinking straight champagne instead of Mimosas because these days it's not the bubbly that causes Acid Reflux, it's the orange juice. But I danced like a fool, so I'd call it a draw on the Old Fartometer.

Then came the golf tournament. I know, you're wondering who would be dumb enough to ask me to join a team that hoped to win a golf tournament. Well it turns out that this was the Comcast Client Appreciation Golf Tournament and I was the client to be appreciated. I was paired with my equally non-athletic account rep but brought two ringers with me for the foursome. In fact, they were so good that a rumor whipped through the player roster that the only all-women foursome included two semi-pros. That was a good thing because the other two of us were semi-conscious.

Since we played "best ball," my Comcast buddy and I mostly teed off for laughs and retreated to our cart to await the frequent arrival of the adult beverage truck. While our shills made one par or birdie after another, we just enjoyed our cocktails and the bayside scenery.

Frankly, the more Yuengling I consumed, the better golfer (in relative terms) I became. By the 17th hole I whacked the ball like an Amazon, sending it farther than I had ever launched one before. It wasn't until I turned to walk back to the golf cart that I discovered I'd also attempted to remove my hip from its socket. Good lord, where is that beverage cart when you need it. My post game wrap up was an ice bag.

This discomforting reality show was followed two days later by my spouse's birthday celebration. She'd kill me if I failed to note here that as of this birthday she is not, repeat, not, yet a Film Society Senior. This birthday.

Anyway, at dinner, six women and two men consumed enough Chinese food and Saki to feed half of Beijing, then waddled out of the restaurant at 9:45 – and decided to pass up dancing and a night cap. 9:45 on a Saturday night for pity's sake and we all retreated to our respective pre-assisted living residences. Confucius say these people really old.

To be fair though, I felt a little less decrepit the next morning when one of our young boyfriends, sporting a dandy hangover, called to say "I should have gone home when the lesbians did." At least he didn't say old lesbians.

But the final test of my senior citizenhood came yesterday on a bright fall afternoon. The Delaware AIDS walk took place in Rehoboth Beach for the first time and I participated. I suspect, in addition to wanting to raise money for the cause, I was trying desperately to hold back the hands of father time and refute my claim to a $1 break on a movie ticket.

No, I thought, there's still hope. I shall defy the clock.

I raised a lot of money. Let's face it, people donated partly out of sincerity for the cause and partly because the very idea of me voluntarily walking 3.5 miles outside of a shopping mall made them giddy.

Ya know, 3.5 miles is longer than it was in the Mesozoic era. By the time we got half way through, I was panting only slightly less than the Rottweiler behind me. Although my tongue may have been hanging out as far.

On the plus side, I am pleased to note I didn't have to utter the old fart classic "I've fallen and I can't get up."

And the fact that I could get out of bed unaided this morning gave me hope.

I proclaim that I am not yet a total old fart. But as far as the Film Society is concerned let's not let on.

See you at the movies. ▼

November 2008

We got a navigation system for my car. I was determined to holdout, as I didn't get my orienteering badge in Girl Scouts for nothing, but several recent episodes changed my mind.

Two weeks ago we tried to get into Manhattan from upstate, missed a turn and traveled all five boroughs before finding the 59th Street Bridge. We were not Feelin' Groovy. (Gen X-ers, tell me you get that reference, please...).

Then I got confused returning from western Delaware and wound up driving through Gumboro, twice. Once is too much.

So going to New York City two weeks ago, we stopped at Best Buy, bought a GPS Navigation System, plugged it in, stuck the screen up on the dashboard and headed north.

I was a little surprised when the device addressed me with a British accent. Cheerio. The voice was pleasant enough, but told us to exit the parking lot in 3 kilometers. As metric morons, we missed the turn, and Mary Poppins said "recalculating" and gave us more directions we couldn't follow. At this rate we'd be circling Piccadilly Circus until Thursday.

Right then and there I should have looked in the book to find out how to emigrate Sarah Ferguson over the pond but I get carsick if I read when we're moving, and Bonnie was busy missing the I-95 ramp three consecutive times.

"Ignore her," I said to Bonnie, "here's the exit." The voice corrected me, saying "re-cal-cu-la-ting. Turn in four kilometers." Jane Austen was a more irritating back seat driver than I was.

When we pulled off for lunch, she seemed a tad annoyed. I tried to make amends by telling her we were stopping for a spot of tea and sticky pudding.

It was getting back on the turnpike that was sticky. Emma Thompson sent us around our elbows to get to our thumbs, in between the diesel pumps and exhaust spewing 18-wheelers. When we followed our instincts instead of her directions I swear it was a testy Margaret Thatcher denouncing us. "Re-cal-cu-la-ting you dumb Yankees...."

Finally, I pushed "menu" and hired an American navigator. Her voice was more casual, but no less irritated when we ignored her. At least we knew how many tenths of a mile we'd gone before missing a turn.

By the Newark New Jersey airport we looked for the Holiday Inn. Although our date was in Manhattan, this was the closest room we could get because of the NY Marathon.

"Turn right at ramp in three quarters of a mile," said Miss America. I clearly saw the hotel off to the left. We exited, and GPS lady told us to turn right. "But it's off to the left," I told Bonnie. "Turn right in two tenths of a mile," said Amelia Earhart, the dashboard bully. "No! Turn left!" I said.

"I can't argue with both of you at once," yelled Bonnie, who then went the wrong way on a one way street in what looked to be gang turf. "Recalculating, Recalculating, Recalculating." By this time the arrow on the navigational device screen channeled a Miró painting.

By the time we found the Holiday Inn again we'd gone round Robin Hood's barn, back an exit on the turnpike and slightly insane. Are we in Wasilla, Alaska yet??? (God, forbid.)

As we parked and got out, Bonnie reminded me to put the GPS in the glove box like the salesman suggested. I considered leaving her in plain view for the opportunity to drive a criminal crazy.

Later, on the way into the City, my city, mind you, where I grew up and knew pretty much every route to everywhere on its easily numbered streets, we obeyed Dora the Explorer again and missed the Holland Tunnel entirely. Not, by the way, easy to do.

Dashboard girl recalculated, taking us through lovely Jersey City, past the rear end of the Statue of Liberty and, after a few weird turns, to our destination – the annual Women's Gala for the New York Gay & Lesbian Community Center. Though the party was at the Chelsea Piers along the Hudson

River, the navigation screen showed the car on 11th Avenue at a falafel stand.

But we got to the gala, where the guests of honor were Lisa Sherman (head of LOGO network, and the spectacular speaker at last year's Rehoboth Beach Women's Conference) and Ilene Chaiken, creator of *The L Word* TV series, and several of its cast members.

Amid flowing cosmos and a dazzling dinner, several speeches touched me, but it was a breathtakingly moving speech by *L Word's* breathtakingly beautiful Jennifer Beall that made me cry. Here was a straight woman, who played gay for Hollywood, choked up about having a chance to help educate America about equality for her gay friends. And with the series ending this Spring, she's saddened that her on-screen opportunity to do so is ending. But off-screen we've got a friend for life. Bonnie got to shake Jennifer Beall's hand, and hated to wash her hands after that.

I wanted to wash my hands of the GPS device, but Bonnie lobbied to give her another chance. Aiming for the airport Holiday Inn again, our directionally challenged electronic gadget sent us to arrivals, departures, air freight and a single toll booth twice, once in each direction, before honing in on the motel.

The next morning, on the return trip, we kept one eye on the road and one ear on the bitch on the dashboard. She did pretty well on the major roads, but much of Delaware baffled her completely (and I have to admit, I get that way sometimes myself). Naturally, she'd never even heard of our street. Approaching home we heard her say "satellite reception lost. Satellite reception lost." And the screen showed us driving off the Nassau Bridge. It was all I could do to keep from tossing the electronic device off the bridge with us.

I'm not saying I'm giving up. It's worth persevering to avoid being an episode of *Lost* through Gumboro and hearing banjo music. But just in case, I'm buying a new atlas. You can never be too rich, too thin or too low-tech.▼

January 2009

Everybody I know told me I was nuts, but I went to the inaugural. I simply had to be there. And it was 39 hours of chaos you can believe in.

My friend Ronni (who had flown in from Ft. Lauderdale) and I started out at 7:30 a.m. the day before the inaugural, driving to my son Eric's house on the fringe of Capitol Hill in D.C.

He'd scared us with worries they'd close bridges and highways at a certain point and we'd be shut out–hence the 0-dark-30 departure, stoked with coffee, prepared for traffic.

Hardly. Although we did see numerous khaki-dressed men stopping all trucks, searching for terrorists in truck bombs. But we arrived safely, without incident.

"Let's buy our souvenirs today," I said, not wanting to carry crap in the Tuesday throng. The whole world had the same idea. At Union Station all the shops, no matter their regular stock, sold souvenirs and it was only marginally less lethal than Walmart on Black Friday. People, myself included, grabbed inaugural branded pins, buttons, hats, shirts, mugs, and golf balls (really) and stood in long cashier lines stretching into the massively crowded station mall. It would have looked like the bloody railroad station scene in *Gone with the Wind* but none of us had room to be laid out.

Schlepping our goodies, we endured the crammed Metro train and headed for Safeway to buy Depends diapers. You heard me.

Eric and I, contemplating the equation of people divided by porta-potties, panicked. More on this later, like that's any reason to keep reading.

At 5 p.m., we headed for Dupont Circle, because Kate Clinton had announced she'd be at gay ground zero Monday evening saging (sage-ing?) the evil spirits out of Washington

105

with this shaman endorsed herb. There she was, waving a burning torch of sage, with a thousand people cheering. As far as I'm concerned there's not enough Lysol, never mind sage, to clean up the stench from the last eight years, but they tried. There was also a 30 ft. high inflatable George Bush at this street party and we were urged to throw shoes at it. People lined up.

From Dupont we headed for dinner in Chinatown, dodging the flood of happy hometown entrepreneurs selling buttons, hats and shirts. At the Metro I had a goosebump moment, as a lone saxophone player stood by the exit, slowly wailing "America the Beautiful." The swarms applauded, smiled, tossed money. After the inaugural, that horn player probably had enough dough for a Ferrari.

Later, friends took us to a gay bar featuring a Fabulous First Ladies Drag Show. The club's music throbbed while a huge video wall showed George Bush making unflattering faces, with superimposed words flashing "Bush's Last Day!!!!"

The first ladies excelled, getting the costuming and lip sync right, if not the gender or often the ethnicity. We drank Bye-Bye-Cheney shooters, so I can't tell you much about the rest of the night. I do know that Ronni and I were probably the oldest people in the room, but we didn't care.

6 a.m. came up pretty fast. Depends time. Eric and I opened the package and looked at the elastic waisted paper garments. Whoa. We discussed whether, if the need desperately arose, we would actually be able to just, um...let go along Pennsylvania Avenue. Didn't think so and relegated the Depends to "a good idea in theory." We'd take our chances.

Then we dressed for the weather, which was, at the moment 18 degrees out. Our anti-hypothermia gear included long underwear, jeans, shirts, sweatshirts with hoods, ear muffs, heavy coats and gloves with those shake-'em-up chemical hand warmers inside. My final armor: ski pants. We could hardly walk, looking like little round South Park cartoons, waddling toward the Capitol.

I have never, ever, seen so many people in one place in my life. And we weren't even to the Mall yet. The streets teemed with humanity, flowing towards the festivities like spawning salmon. Throng, mass, multitude, horde, all in a line 35 people wide, and several city blocks long, stretching toward one of the security tents for entry to the Mall. It was bitter cold. And nobody moved. Not in front of us, not in back of us, and only occasionally someone fought their way side to side, either to get in or more likely get out. We stood chastising ourselves for not coming earlier until the women in front us said she'd been standing in this same place since 5:30 a.m.

Then we began to hear that even ticket holders were being turned away because the Mall was full (full? It's not a stomach, it's the National Mall!). And of course, we were ticketless.

"I refuse to miss this thing!" I said to myself and anybody else who would hear, which would be nobody because of all the earmuffs. I know Ronni was thinking that she left 75 degree Florida to freeze her tush for nothing.

"Let's walk up to the other end of the Mall by the Lincoln Memorial," said Eric as he grabbed my hand and I grabbed Ronni's and we elbowed our way out of the crush.

So we walked and walked, feet freezing, teeth chattering, until we came upon a short line in front of the Greene Turtle Sports Bar on 8th Street. "When does the restaurant open?" I asked the first person in line." "Eleven o'clock," she said. Glances were exchanged.

We cued up at 10:15 and waited 45 minutes while chatting up the gang, politely ignoring Inaugural schmutz peddlers, and ticking off the moments until toilet access. Didn't need diapers after all, although it was close. Between the ski pants, and the rest of my ensemble I felt like Gypsy Rose Lee, and worried I'd have heat stroke before I could disrobe.

Barack Obama took the oath of office as we watched the historic Inaugural from a table in front of five jumbo TV screens, all the while warming up, drinking beer, eating burgers and talking with the wonderful people around us. People chanted

"Yes We Can!" We cheered, sang with Aretha (I'll leave it to others to discuss her hat) and enjoyed every single patriotic, tearful, joyous moment, in a deliciously diverse crowd.

When the helicopter lifted off with *former President Bush* (three of the best words in the English language), Eric led the whole restaurant in a chorus of Shah, nah, nah, nah, hey, hey, good bye."

As for the parade, Anderson Cooper reported a crowd ten deep along the route, so we opted to walk another 28 blocks (!) to Dupont Circle to watch it with friends and thaw out in their cozy, toasty condo.

We bid a fond farewell to Eric around 7:30 p.m., and arrived back home at 10 p.m. Bonnie, who opted out of the trip because just *seeing* crowds on TV gives her claustrophobia, greeted us with relief and a barrage of questions.

"Well, how was it?" she asked.

"Indescribable," I said, "although I guess I'll have to try in my *Letters from CAMP Rehoboth* column.

Indescribably wonderful. Especially since I got to have the group experience without the group hypothermia. Cue the sax with America the Beautiful.▼

February 2009

We got a Wii. If you don't know what that is you are older than I am, which is sad.

Bonnie said she wanted the snazzy video sports games because it would be good exercise. I know she just wanted to play. This is a woman who celebrated her 40th birthday on a roller coaster and spent most of the following decade still squatting behind home plate. While other folks were getting first colonoscopies, she celebrated age 50 speeding along the wrong side of a winding road in the English countryside. The rest of us in the car wanted to see sheep, but not splayed on the windshield. Bonnie and the sheep survived that birthday.

For Bonnie's 60th she wants to do a zip line. I'm lucky I can still zip my pants.

So we got a Wii, no easy task itself. The Big Box Store was always out of the big box of Wii. Then we heard rumor of a truck arriving the next morning.

"I can't believe you're making me get up at 6 in the morning to stand in line at Walmart for my own Hanukah present," Bonnie hissed at me, as I pulled the covers over my head.

"Pretend it's a game," I said.

So she put on her cleats and jockeyed for position as the sun came up over the Walmart parking lot. When the terrified greeter opened the doors my spouse was first off the starting block and I am proud to say she came in by a nose to the electronics department without trampling anybody.

So we got a Wii.

The first time I Wii'd as an adult it was at a friend's house, where I was tapped to go Wii bowling with three former PE teachers. Oddly, I could simulate in the living room what eluded me in the bowling alley and, strike after spare after strike, I beat the pants off all three women. They smiled, but I know these jocks were humiliated to beaten by a klutz like me.

I should have retired my Wii controller and jersey number right then and there.

But now, in our home bowling alley, I roll on, standing in front of the TV, swinging the game controller, and letting go of the button to throw the bowling ball. It's a lot lighter than a real bowling ball, you can't get your thumb stuck in the socket and you don't have to wear somebody else's stinky bowling shoes. Then again, getting athlete's foot is the closest I come to being an athlete.

You do get to hear the delightful echo of bowling balls being mowed down. Wii sound effects rock. And there is applause for strikes. I love applause.

Of course, every time I pick up the controller, Bonnie begs me to secure the wrist band, certain I will eventually launch the device through the 42-inch flat screen Sony.

The good news is that gutter balls are much harder to execute with Wii than in reality. The bad news is dropping your hand too far without releasing the button sends the virtual ball rolling behind you into the cartoon crowd, who scream and sneer at you. I remember that all too well from high school.

And speaking of cartoons, my favorite part of Wii is putting together the cartoon characters resembling you and your friends. There are choices of eyes, ears, noses, hair, eyeglasses, the works. I love that you have no choice of thighs, boobs or butts and everyone looks similar from the neck down. This is not a reality show.

So far, the most Wii fun I've had is cross-dressing my friends and endowing them with inappropriate eyebrows and facial hair.

Last week we invited friends over so we could replicate them into little cartoon avatar figures and have a tournament. I was in the midst of throwing a ten pin split when I put a little too much oomph behind it and pulled a groin muscle. In my living room, in front of the TV. That's a new one.

After bowling, Bonnie challenged me to softball, where she got to throw the ball at ninety miles an hour and I got to flail wildly and miss it. Flashbacks of summer camp. Bonnie now has a right biceps like Popeye's and my rotator cuff is unglued.

Then there's golf. You are supposed to hold the controller like a golf club, but we've not figured out how to do that without squatting and looking like Quasimodo. Hunched and ready, it turns out I'm just as lousy at Wii golf as I am on the course. Although, the way the game is set up, you can only take a certain number of strokes before a disembodied voice tells you to "give up." If somebody told me that in 2005 I could have saved myself a lot of humiliation, not to mention greens fees.

Part of Wii golf is to read the greens, looking at differing shades of the color green to determine the angle of the terrain. Please. I can't even tell my blue turtlenecks from the black ones anymore. Six shades of video green are just cruel.

I've yet to try Wii tennis because I watched Bonnie virtually smashing the ball over the net and figured, first, since it takes two hands, I'd have to put my drink down, and second, it looked like too much exercise. The only thing my backhand is good for is to give compliments.

Now that it's nearly Spring, Bonnie wants to get the new Wii Fit exercise routine. If she makes me participate I might have to throw a wee fit to get out of it. I understand you enter your vital statistics, including your weight and the little cartoons are drawn to more realistically reflect each participant. Can't wait.

The game checks your Body Mass Index, tells you your Wii Fit age and keeps tabs on your weight. Let's face it, Wii might want to be fit, but there's no way Wii (the Royal Wii) are having any part of that.

As Bonnie says, "Wii shall see about that…"

Wii shall overcome?. ▼

Schnauzerhaven was invaded by an alien. Undocumented, but she did have papers. All over the house. We babysat for a puppy.

Frankly, my dogs, my spouse and I never knew how old we all were until our twenty one days on puppy watch. Actually it was only three days, but it felt like dog years.

First, the visitor was not a Schnauzer-American, which immediately alerted my terrier immigration squad. She was a ball of white fur with a floppy tail – something else very foreign – and entirely relentless. Running, rolling, crouching, kissing, snuggling, sniffing, peeing, pooping. For the puppy Olympics we didn't lead with a torch, but thought about torching the house by closing ceremonies.

You should have seen my 11-year-old dog cavort with the puppy. They crouched, facing off, butts high, circling, then running outside, lapping the back yard twice and racing back towards the porch. As the puppy crossed the finish line, the oldster stopped to lie down. I swear I heard him ask for an Aleve.

When 10-year-old Paddy turned his back on the pup, she took it as a challenge and nipped at him until he agreed to grab the soggy end of a rawhide bone. The two of them ran around the house, each with an end of the rawhide in their mouths until Ms. Puppy ran under the bed and Paddy got clocked in the head for being too tall to fit. I swore I heard him ask for an Aleve.

In the meantime, another Schnauzer relative of the boys arrived for a sleepover, setting up a classic three dog night plus the interloper. It's 11 p.m. Do you know where your canines are? Just about everywhere.

We had Paddy the Jealous under the covers mid-bed and Ashley the Rotund up top between the pillows, with Penny the

Puppy lying where my feet should have gone. Moxie the Elder retreated to his doggie bed escape module on the floor.

I've had a better night's sleep in U.S. Airways Coach.

Although "night's sleep" is inaccurate. Cirque du Soleil began at 4 a.m., long before Soleil rise. Usually, I can sneak out of bed, go to the bathroom and be back under the covers without blowing reveille. But this time, when my feet hit the floor they were followed by sixteen paws and a chorus of yapping. You can tell a 10-year-old dog to shut up and go back to sleep, but tell that to a puppy and you'll be tip-toeing through turd tulips in the morning.

So we all got up and went out. Now here's the thing about the puppy. She doesn't come when called. Or sit on command, or do anything else requested of her by any human. Dog trainer Caesar Milan needs to give her an extreme makeover.

It's a good thing those Cypress trees surrounding my house are good and thick. Passing motorists should not have had to look over the fence to witness two women of a certain age loping around the yard, clad only in our t-shirts and underpants, trying to lure said puppy back into the house.

Finally, when everybody was indoors, we divided the troops. Bonnie bunked on the sofa with one Schnauzer and the Puppy from Hell, while I retreated to bedroom headquarters with the other two. It didn't stay that way long because while I nodded off, one canine must have grown opposable thumbs and managed to open the bedroom door. The pack ran back and forth for what was left of the night, popping up and down on the bed like Whack-a-Moles.

When we finally gave up trying to sleep, I got dressed and left for work. Bonnie, who goes in later than I do had an easy time getting the regulars into their crates. Not the puppy. The little devil ran under the bed and Bonnie crouched down to coax her out. The puppy crawled on her belly to the far side of the bed, so Bonnie stood up, walked around to the far side, squatted and called the puppy. That's when the infuriating little creature reversed gears and retreated to the original side of the bed. Bonnie walked around and crouched, the puppy fled; Bonnie changed sides, so did the pup. Staggering to her feet, my mate concluded that the squat and run dance could go on all day so she gave up and took an Aleve.

The three caged Schnauzers spent the day watching a perfectly good carpet being defiled by the fuzzy weapon of mass destruction.

By that afternoon we were all really dragging except, of course, you-know-who. Yet another Schnauzer dropped by for a few hours of doggy daycare, so now there were four mature dogs being chased around the house by a six pound nipper. She was so determined to sniff every butt in the house (except mine and Bonnie's thank god), I was afraid one of the dogs would stop short, with the resulting rear end collision turning the puppy into a pug.

The next morning, feeding the pack presented its own problems. We separated the bowls to the four corners of the kitchen. One with puppy chow, one with weight loss kibble for seniors, another with lamb and rice kibble for sensitive stomachs and the last a kibble and green bean happy meal.

Well, nobody was happy. They each wanted what the other one was having and we humans had to stand guard, keeping everybody out of everybody else's business, no easy task with dogs or humans.

After breakfast, since the sky had turned black, we all went back to bed. There was a succession of lightning bolts, followed immediately by some of the loudest, most frightening thunder since last Tuesday's Rush Limbaugh show.

En masse, the dog pack leapt onto the bed, shaking and quaking from fear. They had the mattress jiggling so much from the panting vibrations I felt like I'd just put a quarter into the bed in some sleazy motel.

Just before it was time for puppy love to go home, I had a panic attack. I counted noses and hers was missing. I knew we hadn't opened any doors, I had seen her just moments before, but a thorough canvass turned up nothing but Schnauzers. We called, we looked under beds, we peered into closets (nobody there except a few Republican politicians) and searched like Google. No puppy.

Frantic, I paced to the coffee table to grab the remote to turn the TV off–I wanted to hear Penny if she made a noise. As I picked up the remote, I peered through the glass coffee table to the shelf below. There, between the pile of gift books and a stack of DVDs slept one tired little puppy. Adorable when asleep.

She's gone home now. All visiting Schnauzers have departed as well. We're down to our happy household of two humans, two dogs. I'm sure that if enough time elapses we will be up for puppy duty again. Make that puppy doody. I just found a souvenir in the corner.

I need an Aleve. ▼

FLOUNDERING ON THE HIGH SEAS

"You can't swing a cat in Rehoboth without hitting a lesbian."

The quote, quite true, came from a group of gay gals laughing it up along Baltimore Avenue last week in the incredible sunshine and heat. April? Town was packed!

And as one of those in danger of being smacked in the head with a flying feline, it's just great to see the weather change for the good here in Gayberry RFD. The April taste of summer wasn't wasted on me. Having been cooped up most of the winter, nose to the computer keyboard, I immediately put the convertible top down on my car and drove around town like a tourist. Upon my return to the house I flung open the windows and luxuriated in the fresh scent of cherry tree flowers and blooming plants.

What was I thinking? After one night's sleep with open windows, I had two pounds of pollen packed in my sinus cavities and another bushel blanketing every surface in the house. I'm sniffling and snorting from allergies that feel like swine flu. I tried a sinus wash – you know, waterboarding, like the military uses for torture. It didn't help.

Then, like fools we went to the nursery for the annual replacement plants. I don't know why we don't just stick plastic flowers in the planters. If all the dollar bills I spend each spring replacing dead stuff were laid end to end they'd reach to the condominium I should be living in.

We toted plants sentenced to death to a car covered in pollen, for planting in a yard that's basically a dog latrine. Tomorrow we'll plant the greenery on death row, I mean the backyard. Achoo!

A glutton for punishment, Bonnie and I then accepted an invitation to breathe in several more buckets of pollen and allergens – we went for a day on Rehoboth Bay, fishing. I've never been a fisherperson, news that I'm sure shocks you.

But much to my delight though, the generous Captain and First Mate surprised me with my very own fishing rod – pink, with teeny sparkly lights that blinked whenever the reel spun. "I couldn't resist," said the Captain. I think it was the Hannah Montana edition.

After drifting for a while near the Indian River Bridge, me with my pink fishing pole dangling professionally from the side of the boat as I busied myself with e-mail on my phone, the first mate landed a big flounder. Mission (dinner) accomplished. We reeled in to go traveling.

This is where it got interesting.

On our way out of the Indian River Inlet and into the ocean, Bonnie and I sat up front on the speedy fishing boat. I may be a neophyte fisherperson, but I'm an experienced boater, having lived on and traveled in a 29 foot power boat all around the Delaware and Chesapeake Bays, up to New York City and Fire Island and back. The alternate title of my first book was going to be *My Life as Ballast*.

So imagine my surprise when, as we nosed out toward the ocean, what I can only describe as a mighty rogue wave swelled up in front of the boat and made my eyeballs switch sockets.

(FREEZE FRAME)

This gigantic wall of water rose in a colossal swell about, I don't know, a thousand feet higher than the boat deck. Okay, six feet overhead and five feet away. I channeled Shelley Winters, picturing that fierce wave crashing through the cockpit windows on the Poseidon. I marveled at the wave's enormity, its stark green expanse of color, with bubbling white foam on top. I gasped when I saw two more identical waves right behind it. I went into a momentary coma, broken only by the sound of somebody screaming. It was me.

(ACTION!)

With a giant crash, the wall of water hit the boat, the bow

rose to conquer it and we thumped up, then down like a bathtub toy. Geeze it was scary, seeing all that dark water up close and wondering, omigod, is the nose of the boat going to come back up again?.

(FREEZE FRAME)

If the bow didn't come back up it was called pitch-poling – "*pitch·poled, pitch·pol·ing, pitch·poles* Nautical. To flip or cause to flip end over end." I learned the term in Power Squadron boating class, or, as I used to call it, *101 Ways to Drown* or *Blow Up Your Boat*. I know they wanted to frighten us into caution, but they scared the barnacles out of us – and I was flashing back to pitch-pole class. And of course it didn't help in the pitch-pole department that it was my lard ass sitting up front as, once again, ballast.

(ACTION!)

Of course the bow came back up, but we got a thundering, frigid shower. It may have been 90 degrees out but the ocean didn't get the memo.

When we looked back at the captain, who was hollering a reassuring "We're okay, don't worry…" the second wave pounded us, sending a fresh freezing tsunami into the boat, then a third. We got glacial facials and held an impromptu wet t-shirt contest. This was now a combination of fishing and a sinus wash.

Amazingly, as soon as the Captain turned left up the coast, the water went calm again.

Alrighty now. I was drenched, hoping it was all sea water and I hadn't peed myself. The Captain and First Mate were pretty wet, too. But Bonnie really got the worst of it. She was dripping wet from head to toe and I expected to see her wearing a flounder on her head.

Three of us sopped off with towels, but Bonnie was undryable. She shed her shorts and shirt, wrapped up in a towel and noted it would be an inopportune time to be stopped by vacationing Somali pirates. We laughed and hooted and hollered. Lucky for me, my Disney fishing pole survived the incident.

(FREEZE FRAME)

Really, we were freezing our frames but the sun shone, dolphins swam by, we cruised along and waved to the crowds on the beach. How lucky to be invited for a wonderful cruise in the sunshine. Achoo! The season had begun and all was right with the world.

(ACTION!)

Now I'm off to close up the house, turn on the A/C, and over-water the plants. ▼

I was at Our Lady of Lowes last Sunday morning along with much of the other lesbian population of Sussex County when I spied two friends walking down the aisle with what appeared to be a birdhouse.

Oh no, they said, it was a bat house and it's all the rage now for clearing backyards of mosquitoes. Every lesbian they know is putting up a bat house.

Now I'm as anxious as the next person to avoid B-52 mosquito squads, but the idea of inviting bats to the party to deter mosquitoes seemed rather like inviting Dick Cheney over for hot dogs in order to keep Colin Powell away. I'd rather have General Powell and a swarm of blood-sucking mosquitoes than Dick Cheney and bats. Dick Chaney and bats, in the same sentence, that's quite appropriate.

No, no, said my friends, bats are lovely guests, you hardly see them and they insure a swarm-free picnic on the deck. They are nature's best insect deterrent. To me, nature's best insect deterrent is staying in the house.

Next, my buds told me you have to mount the bat house on a twelve foot pole, which I agreed was perfect as I wouldn't touch anything to do with bats with a ten foot pole. My spouse just rolled her eyes and put a bat house into our shopping cart. Peer pressure sucks.

So I did some research. All you have to do to attract bats is to provide them with a bat-friendly structure. Apparently bats like crowded, warm spaces, so we're lucky we don't attract them to women's happy hour on Friday night. And they like it to be 80 to 100 degrees where they can bask in the sun. Perhaps they'd like an Olivia cruise.

Experts suggest putting a thermometer atop the pole along with the bat house so you can check if the temperature is right to attract occupants. I can barely stagger to the TV in the morning to check the weather channel, so there's very little chance of me shimmying up a pole to check the bat climate.

Here's good news: "a single brown bat can eat up to 1,000 mosquitoes in one hour." I imagine that a single gray schnauzer can eat one bat in the time it takes for me to hit them both with a broom to break up the feast. This concerns me.

"A single bat consumes up to 3000 insects a night – a third of those are usually mosquitoes!" Good god, what are the other two thirds, locusts?

"Bats kill mosquitoes that spread West Nile Virus." Oy, something else I never worried about that I can obsess over now.

Here's a great fact. In Austin, Texas there's a place called Bracken Cave, which is the summer home to between… ready…20 to 30 million Mexican free-tailed bats. Like I needed another reason never to go to Texas.

On the internet I found a pamphlet called Attracting Bats, which, along with Field Guide to Moose Dressing is something I figured I never would have to read. Apparently, using lures like bat guano doesn't work, thank god. Did I ever think I'd be typing the words "bat guano?"

Holy Bat Box Batman, this attracting bats thing is much like field of nightmares – build it and they will come. Eventually. We should have put the bat box up this past spring, before the bats came back from their winter hibernation. That's good, actually, since Bonnie can have all the fun in the world installing it now and I won't have to worry about going bats for at least a year. Now that's a project I can encourage. I bet the bats hibernate in Ft. Lauderdale like the rest of Rehoboth.

Another bat book warns that it could be three to five years before I get a healthy contingent of bats. At that rate, when we sell the house the bats will convey. This project is sounding better and better.

I wound up on the internet half the night looking at bat stuff. I especially liked the site with advice on getting rid of nuisance bats. At this point in my reading, there seems to be no other kind.

But no, there are a zillion varieties. According to the Bat Conservation Organization you can even sponsor a bat, choosing from big brown bats or Vampire Bats. They even have names, like Gandalf the Egyptian Fruit Bat. I wanted to know whether I would get a welcome kit and wallet-sized picture of Gandalf if I sponsored him. Can we e-mail and get updates? Is my sponsorship enough to feed and clothe a bat for a year?

I made the mistake of posting my little bat project on Facebook and immediately started getting all kinds of dire warnings.

Most began with, "Are you crazy???," followed by the advice that building a house for Purple Martins would work just as well against mosquitoes. Then somebody suggested I forget the Purple Martins and go directly for purple martinis which suited me fine. I could get back to the bat project later.

But then came the most dire warning of all. "Careful! They love coming in the house – and I don't mean the mosquitoes! Ever try catching one as it fly dives from room curtain to room curtain? We did – finally had to call a bat catcher to do the job."

Okay, now I'm picturing having to call Dracula Exterminators for a bat geek to prowl around my darkened house with a giant fish net while the dogs and I check into a motel.

That did it. I sent Bonnie, the bat house and the twelve foot pole back to Lowes with instructions to return with Citronella candles and Deep Woods Off. I'm relieved there won't be bats at Schnauzerhaven any time soon, but I'm seriously worried about all those lesbians in Rehoboth trying to lure bats into their belfries. Give it up, girls. Maybe this summer, to get up close and personal with bats, we should skip the Michigan Womyns's Music Festival and go to the Annual Great Lakes Bat Festival on August 28 and 29. At this one, I hope to hell nobody gets naked in the woods.

Now I'm off to get a purple martini.▼

June 2009

For me, last week may have been the gayest week ever.

We visited NYC to attend a fundraiser and have a **gay** old time (adj. "having or showing a merry, lively mood"). First stop, Chelsea Pines Inn, the **gay** (adj. "indicating or supporting homosexual interests") B&B operated by my delightfully **gay** (noun. "A male homosexual") high school boyfriend.

While waiting in our **gaily** (adj.) adorned room, before meeting our **gay** (noun) son for cocktails, we flipped on the TV to find Turner Movie Classics playing Judy Garland's *Meet Me in St. Louis*. How **gay** is *that*? (Okay, I have no idea what part of speech covers that one).

On Saturday night we had drinks at The Ritz lounge, saw the spectacular gay-themed play *Next Fall*, and wound up at gay ground zero, Christopher Street, to kick off the 40th anniversary celebration of the Stonewall Inn Rebellion. There's something about standing in a dark, dingy piano bar, surrounded by a hundred musical theatre queens and belting out "Oklahoma!" that positively screams GAY!!!!!!!!!!!!!.

The bar, Marie's Crisis, has been there for over 35 years and quite possibly the gin-soaked piano player has been there that long as well. It's the only kind of place I can "sing out, Louise" without fear of sending listeners into seizures.

But Sunday evening held the weekend's signature event: Broadway Bares – the 19th annual fundraiser for Broadway Cares/Equity Fights AIDS. The collective chorus boys and girls from all the Broadway musicals rehearsed for months on their days off putting together this giant burlesque show. The dancing, singing, costumes and lights, fabulous as they were, took a back seat to the buff, beautiful bodies, male and female, stripping, teasing and showing off their um, assets. Charitable giving has never been such fun.

Recuperating back home in Rehoboth after all this gay

culture, we switched gears from fundraising to activism.

Finally, after 13 long years of painful and futile efforts, a bill (SB 121) to add the words "sexual orientation" to Delaware's anti-discrimination statute seemed poised to pass in the Senate on Tuesday, June 23. By doing an end-run around some anti-gay legislators, the plan envisioned the bill passing in the Senate, with our Representative Pete Schwartzkopf ready to run it across the hall, suspend House rules and take it up instantly for passage.

Man plans, God laughs. It was an end-run alright. As I was on the way to Dover for the 2 p.m. session I received a call that the President Pro Tem of the Senate, Thurman Adams, the man who'd locked the bill in his desk drawer for years, passed away mere hours before the bill was to have its hearing. Forgive me, the old coot said it would pass over his dead body, and....

Suffice it to say, we feared he'd managed to scuttle the bill once more, this time from the great beyond.

Fear not, Senator Sokola and Representative Schwartzkopf managed to reschedule the bill for 3 p.m. the next day.

Readers, you are lucky you weren't there. The opposition attached three ugly amendments to the bill, essentially saying that the bill would make it illegal to discriminate based on sexual orientation unless individuals or businesses had deeply held religious beliefs against homosexuality, and then it would be fine to discriminate. Really. Passage with that amendment would be worse than having no protection at all. The right to discriminate against gay people would be the law of the land.

We sat in the Senate hearing, listening to four miserable hours of insulting, mean-spirited, ignorant testimony from a handful of legislators and their witnesses, favoring this and other heinous amendments.

Since it's 2009, not 1999, our unworthy opponents felt compelled to compliment gay people as good tax-paying citizens, even calling some of us their friends, before trying to stuff their religious values down everyone's throats.

Frankly, I liked it better when bigots were out of the closet. It would have been easier to listen to folks in white hoods saying, "I hate homosexuals so we shouldn't enact this bill." At times I found myself gnawing on my knuckles to keep from screaming.

I also blogged on Facebook:

- *Killed one amend of three. Keep u posted.*

- *A woman with "a Christian bakery," whatever that is, says she should have the right to refuse to bake a cake for a gay wedding.*

- *Killed second stupid amendment.*

- *Now Sen.Venables is yammering that "lesbians can be made." Gay men, not so much. What the hell does that mean?*

- *I wish I had a catheter.*

- *If a student has two mommies, there's a yutz saying that the school should not even acknowledge it.*

- *My god, these people are scared that protecting gays from being fired will lead to teachers being instructed to teach tots about homosexual sex. I'm practicing abstinence—I'm not shrieking!!!!!*

- *Three amendments down and roll call to go*

- *Bill passes in senate! 14 YES, 5 NO.*

- *Get me to the ladies room!!!!!!*

- Pete called House back into session. Same crappy amendments introduced.

- *Another hour of ridiculous hate speech.*

- *Spooky: the rain outside just stopped and a giant rainbow is over Legislative Hall. Somebody saying "not so fast" to those ugly amendments? Judy come to help?*

- *It passed!!!! 26 YES, 14 No. Tears of joy! We've been sitting through this battle for 13 years. I just congratulated Pete Schwartzkopf for being an incredible advocate and a man of his word.*

- *Over and out, kids!*

So gay people in Delaware are now protected in employment, housing and public accommodations. That's a relief. I hope the religious bigots know that the bill also protects them from being discriminated against for their peculiarly hurtful religious views.

Saturday was the capper on the gayest week ever. The Delaware Stonewall Democrats hosted a joyous party celebrating the 40th anniversary of the 1969 Stonewall Inn Rebellion that launched the gay rights movement. Governor Jack Markell attended, made moving remarks and announced his commitment to sign the anti-discrimination bill at CAMP Rehoboth the following Thursday.

Thanks to Governor Markell, our wonderfully supportive legislators, and everyone who has worked to make this happen for 13 long years.

Great day. Great week.

I am very, very gay (noun and adjective). ▼

July 2009

I'm being followed. All the time. I feel like I'm in Witness Protection, with the mob gunning for me. In fact, I know exactly who is following me and to date there are 157 of them – just waiting to know what I am doing every single moment. It's scary.

Who's guessed? Ta-da! I am Twittering!

FayJRB: It's July 5. I have laryngitis. Why is everyone laughing?

Now if you have been under a large rock for the last year, or simply go catatonic at the mention of 21st century technology, here's a primer.

Twitter is a communications network – minus anchors, commercials, studios or high definition. Best of all, no talking heads come uninvited into your living room.

Mary Matalin and Rush can stand in a forest and Twitter, but thank goodness, to me it doesn't make a sound.

FayJRB: I am sitting, covered in hard-shell crab debris, picking crab meat.

Is this something inquiring minds want to know???? Joining Twitter means developing a network of twits you want to follow and see which twits want to follow you back. Oh, and the tweets you write are only allowed to be 140 characters long and are only allowed to answer a single question: "What are you doing?"

FayJRB: Oh, crap, I'm wiping Old Bay seasoning off my Blackberry.

Twitter allows you to fritter away your day twittering. Everybody's Clark Kent at the *Daily Planet*. Not only are people living their lives, but they are tweeting about them in real time.

Now it's one thing to tweet "I'm at Aqua drinking a Cosmo" and entirely another to tweet "I'm driving 45 mph around the circle on Rehoboth Avenue." I have seen this scary thing–a moving car with the driver balancing an iPhone on the steering wheel and twittering away. Please god let the next tweet say "got pulled over before I killed somebody."

FayJRB: I'm procrastinating. Went to play 9 holes instead of writing my column about Twittering.

Here's what I don't understand. Why should somebody except my editor care if I'm golfing instead of completing my work? Some people use Twitter to give a running commentary on their entire lives. Along with a great big who cares, how can they pay attention to what they are doing while simultaneously tweeting about it?

Back in the early part of this century (2002) I thought that the crawl on the TV while the anchor was talking was distracting. Ha! That's nothing compared to somebody playing hoops and tweeting about the last 2-pointer. This is happening. Maximum multi-tasking.

FayJRB: Got up early to finish column so editor doesn't strangle me.

So just how did I become such a twit? I downloaded something called Tweet Deck, which is not at all like a tape deck, which is, I hear, totally obsolete. In addition, the word Tweeter itself reminds me of Woofers and Tweeters – those parts of your stereo speaker system (I think that whole concept is obsolete as well) that used to be housed in walnut cabinets the size of a dining room table.

No, this is the new kind of tweeter alright and I'm trying to determine if it's for me.

FayJRB: Still have laryngitis and post nasal drip.

Why do I think this was not what the internet or cell phone was invented for? Who cares if I am hacking and coughing and tweeting about it? Does this interest you? Say yes and I will send somebody over with a butterfly net to take you away.

FayJRB: Oops, time for my sinus wash.

Now there's a real scoop for the *New York Times*. This is the kind of thing people are twittering about. Just got a new one. Great, an acquaintance just walked his dog, and the dog did two number ones and one number two. Is this insane, or what?

FayJRB: I'm deciding between my Yankees t-shirt or my "Be careful what you say or you'll end up in my novel t-shirt."

Gee, if this isn't Pulitzer stuff, nothing is. I'm so glad to be using this free social utility to stay connected to other Tweeters in real time. This is need to know stuff.

FayJRB: I'm thinking of heading to the back yard to pick up dog poop.

Yes indeedy, this micro-blogging thing really works for me. I sure enjoy this always-on social network presence. Oh, here's another Tweet for me. Wow, I've got a colleague who just had a bagel with whitefish salad. Quick, call CNN, this is breaking news.

FayJRB: I'm wasting time on Twitter. Nothing is getting done. No column, no laundry, no nothing.

Maybe this Twitter craze will Tweet itself out. Oh good, now six more people are following me to the back yard for scooper duty. FYI, I wish they were actually following me and helping. There's a lot of poop out here...in the yard and out in the Twitosphere.

FayJRB: Twit, here, over and out.▼

MERMAIDS AND SATYRS UNITE!

You know, sometimes I have to grapple for days to think of a topic for this column and sometimes one just falls kerplunk into my lap. So it was this week when I heard about Senator Sam Brownback and his new legislation to ban the creation of half human-half animal hybrids. Where to start?

First off, it's too late. Brownback himself is half-human, half-jackass, so what's the point? But it's hard for me to believe that this Republican anti-stem cell activist is spending his senate time worrying about scientists creating centaurs and mermaids when he really should be worrying about the state of the union.

Hey, Sam, I know there's a lot of talk about hybrids in Washington, but I really don't think they are talking about half-human, half birdbrain. In case you care, it's been done: George Bush.

If you think I am kidding, this is real legislation being proposed by Brownback and 20, count 'em 20, other senators to ban the creation of "part-human, part-animal creatures, which are created in laboratories, and blur the line between species." When it comes to blurring the line between species, Ann Coulter has been blurring the lines between human and cockroach for years.

Truly, you gotta admire the gumption of these legislators to introduce the Human-Animal Hybrid Prohibition Act of 2009. According to Brownback, "Creating human-animal hybrids, which permanently alter the genetic makeup of an organism, will challenge the very definition of what it means to be human and is a violation of human dignity and a grave injustice."

No, a violation of human dignity is marriage inequality in this country while human-stud horse hybrids like Senators Mark Sanford and John Ensign continue to reap the legal benefits of wedded bliss.

I don't know what's so wrong with these mix and match species anyway. You've got the hilarious comic Bruce Vilanch, who is a delightful human-teddy bear hybrid, while on occasion, like at a buffet, I fall into the human-sow category. And who hasn't enjoyed Michelle Pfeiffer as Catwoman?

From what I understand, Brownback got on this kick because of his background in agriculture, working to produce superior snap peas. For him it was a quick jump from frozen vegetables to mermaids and satyrs. The world is full of scary, serious, life-threatening problems, and Brownback is worrying about…mermaids? Bette Midler should sue for defamation.

Okay, I get the mermaid thing. We'd have to be pretty sure they'd come out of the test tube looking like Darryl Hannah and not some icky-sweet Disney creature, but I think it's worth the risk.

And your satyrs – for heaven's sake – Brownback is worried about satyrs? According to mythology, satyrs are half man, half goat, with a love for wine and a huge sexual appetite. This is Rehoboth, people! You've been to the bars. People love our local satyrs!

Gee, we haven't even talked about the half-human, half ostrich. Wouldn't that be Sarah Palin teaching her kids abstinence?

In his own words, Brownback says, "You could make a change now that could be passed along through the gene-pool for the rest of humanity. We do not know what the full effect of this could be." Oh yes we do, look at the gene pool that produced Dick Cheney.

In defending this ridiculous bill, Brownback has said, "What was once only science fiction is now becoming a reality, and we need to ensure that experimentation and subsequent ramifications do not outpace ethical discussion…. History does not look kindly on those who violate the dignity of the human person."

Really? How about violating the dignity of the half-gay, half-soldier? Senator Brownback is so worried about labs producing half man, half sheep, that his entire delegation is willing to act like sheep-men and vote in lock-step against the dignity of the human gay person.

I'm not letting the cat-woman out of the bag here when I tell you that Brownback has long had some pretty weird ideas. He's the guy who wanted to abolish the departments of education, energy and commerce, not to mention what seems like a really fantastic idea now: putting social security money into the stock market. He'd probably have trusted part-human, part-shark Bernie Madoff.

Now this goofball wants to spend our time and money going after mythical creatures. My idea of a mythical creature is a senator who works with both sides of the aisle to actually get something positive done for the taxpayers. Seems as if those are as extinct as dodo birds and minotaurs.

As Brownback says, "The Human-Animal Hybrid Prohibition Act of 2009 works to ensure that our society recognizes the dignity and sacredness of human life."

Puleeze.

But then, the legislation does ban minotaurs. You know, those creatures who are half-man, half-bull. Brownback bans himself. There's a winner. Go for it.▼

July 2009

I'm thrilled about the gayby boom.

When the first real wave of lesbians with child began, I was already on the cusp of menopause so the subject was always pretty academic in my house. That the boom came too late for me and Bonnie, was okay with me. I like kids, I do. It's just that I haven't spent any time around children since they were my peer group.

So frankly, I was quite comfortable in my childless lesbian world. But as the gay parenting trickle turned into a spate and then a boom, it sure has been fun to watch.

Like the time we went to dinner with a couple we'd just met. As the waiter took drink orders, Bonnie and I chose vodka and tonic, one of our new friends asked for a glass of white wine, and our fourth companion looked up at the waiter and said, "Nothing for me, thanks, I just inseminated myself."

The waiter handled it rather nicely. "How about a Shirley Temple?" he asked. Then turned and walked smack into the wall.

Now I don't know about you, but while it may be politically correct for lesbians to have babies, I think Emily Post would say it's still incorrect to discuss insemination at the dinner table.

"Yes," my new friend continued, "It was so weird. I almost got a speeding ticket on the way home tonight. When the cop stopped me I told him I had just been to the sperm bank, and the sperm was in the cooler on the front seat, and I had to get home and inseminate myself, or it would spoil. He let me go."

I bet he did. And I can imagine the conversation later in the squad room.

Also in the "too much information" department came the day we sat at a restaurant and spied two women at the next table, one obviously very pregnant. We smiled at them in a friendly "my-gaydar-is-working kind of way. The pregnant woman looked at us and announced "artificial insemination."

Who asked? It's like the straight couple behind us pointing to their baby and saying "missionary position." No need to know, thank you.

Then we met two women who found a sperm bank just too impersonal for their baby project. But they worried that having a male friend provide the goods might make him feel financially obligated, or worse, lead to parental meddling. So they cooked up a cloak and dagger scheme requiring several male friends to provide twice weekly donations and deliver them surreptitiously.

Each contributor had instructions to drop by the house early in the morning on a rotating schedule of days, open the unlocked front door, sneak up the stairs like a cat burglar and deposit the gift in a Dixie cup on the back of the toilet tank. The women promised to stay in bed with the door closed until they were certain the daily drop had been made.

Voila! There would always be a donation available in case the time was right for basting the turkey.

Several things happened. First, the police began to watch the place, certain it was a crack house.

Second, the schedule occasionally got confused with two donors showing up, samples in tow, bursting into laughter in the darkened stairwell.

Third, everyone began to look like hell. The boys had to get up early and, er...produce, before their morning jogs and the girls had to gauge how long to stay locked in the bedroom before safely going to pee.

Fortunately, sperm and egg met and began the beguine before the guys were hospitalized for exhaustion or the girls got Uremic poisoning.

Sometimes the gayby stories even involved me. I got a surprise once when a favorite male couple came for dinner and one of them said, "We're thinking of having a child, could we rent your womb?" I dropped my spatula into charcoal.

"My uterus is in a jar in somebody's lab," I said, laughing, "You'll have to keep looking. And besides, I suggest you try a puppy first just to see how the Waterford Crystal and Queen Anne furniture hold up."

For the record, they took my advice and stopped at the Shitzu.

But these days, same-sex families are so ubiquitous it's the spawn rather than the parents causing the smiles. And teachers and neighbors are starting to get used to it.

We have acquaintances whose six year old son was asked to write a story in three sentences as his homework. His essay was as follows: My Daddy's friend Mona is a man. Mona dresses up like a woman. Mona is pretty.

I'd love to have been privy to the teacher's reaction, but the essay got a star.

In one household with two men and a four year old, the bedtime admonishment goes ""If you don't behave, there will be no ABBA tonight!" How gay is that!

And while it's way too late for me to join the rent-a-womb brigade or adopt a Chinese baby, I do drive way too fast sometimes. So I'm thinking about keeping a cooler on the front seat.

"You see, officer, I've just been to the sperm bank, and...."▼

August 2009

I'm astounded. Bonnie and I just got back from the Canadian Rockies, where we canoed, white-water rafted and hiked. No, I am not kidding. We hiked way more times than we had cocktails, which is just wrong.

Before the trip I wouldn't have bet ten cents I could have managed all this physical activity – and truthfully, if Larry the vacation planner told us what he was planning I might not have gone, which would have been criminal, since I had a blast.

On our first day in Banff, Canada I got a whiff of the trouble ahead. We rode a cable car up some gorgeous mountains – and from there hiked up to a second, higher observatory. Why did most people have hiking poles and sturdy shoes while I had a digital camera and sandals? At 4000 feet above sea level I gasped for oxygen and my legs burned with each step up. I wanted a hiking pole just to poke Larry in the butt with. I would have bought poles, too, but I was sure this hike would be the only time I needed them. Hah!

The next day we went whitewater rafting on a course advertised as fun for the whole family. Who, the Addams Family? Frankly, this was the most strenuous thing I've ever done. And that was just pulling the wet suit up over my ass.

They gave us all kinds of instructions about what to do if we fell out of the boat and I thought it was hilarious. I mean nobody would fall out, there were pre-teens along. Besides, the way we were costumed, with wet suit, splash jacket, helmet and life vest, none of us could move, much less topple out.

I perched on the side of the inflatable boat, paddling away, smiling and enjoying myself until we hit a five foot drop, the raft twisted and Larry fell out.

Holy crap. As our guide leaned over, grabbed him by the life vest and plunked him back in the boat I realized the severity of my situation.

From that moment on, my right hand clutched a rubber handle in the boat and my wetsuited butt clamped itself onto the inflatable. My behind was so clenched that when we finally got back to shore, I had a hamstring injury and couldn't lift my left leg to get back into the car.

Bonnie, however, unclenched, voluntarily jumped into the icy water for a swim. Opposites attract.

Next on the Olympic schedule came canoeing on a lake so azure blue it looked like a Home Depot paint chip. Now a canoe is an unstable little boat and I'm an unstable big person. Once I sat down in the front I was fine, but getting in was a bit of tippy-canoe and screaming too. Eventually we settled down to a delightfully quiet hour of paddling on a serene lake surrounded by glacier-covered mountains. Amazing.

Then, as told to me, Larry and his canoeing partner returned ahead of us. His buddy removed his life vest but Larry did not. "You're on land now, Larry, you can take off the life jacket."

"Oh no," he said, "I have to help Fay out of the boat and anything can happen." That's what friends are for.

After canoeing, we went to the Banff Hot Springs, soaking in a huge public 104-degree pool surrounded by mountains and Canadians. I asked several Canadians about their health care system and they were all absolutely thrilled with their government-run option. And none of their elderly parents have been ordered killed by government bureaucrats.

In short order we trudged up to some magnificent water-falls, traversing trails dotted with tree roots, ruts and rocks to be scaled, where once again I suffered hiking stick envy. I'd have climbed more comfortably if I was as thin as the air. Coming back we stopped on the roadside to see elk, horned sheep and mountain goats. Western Canada was having a record hot spell and the moose and bear population was cooling off out of sight. Drat, no photo ops.

From Banff we drove on the Icefield Parkway to the Columbia glaciers, where we rode in a mountain climbing vehicle up onto the glacier, where, duh, it was slippery and cold. And impressive and beautiful, albeit disturbing to see the sign in the parking lot noting where the toe of the glacier had been in 1904. What global warming?

Then we were off to the little town of Jasper, and its record heat wave. Did we see any wildlife on the way? Only me when I discovered our cabin lacked air conditioning. That was one miserable night.

But it was better by early morning when we rode the Jasper tramway up 7000 feet to an observatory above town. From there, a bizarrely steep dirt path led to the very top of the mountain.

So far, we'd been hiking at angles far steeper than the ones I'd labeled sadistic on my treadmill. But this one took the cake. I noticed strategically placed boulders all along the path, probably to keep collapsing tourists from falling all the way back down to Jasper. As Bonnie and I huffed and puffed, pulled each other up and rested periodically on the boulders, I was tempted to mug passing climbers for their expensive hiking poles.

Fortunately, Larry had reached the top and was on his way back down when he came upon us, draped over a boulder and gasping for air. We took congratulatory photos that looked like we'd reached the top and headed back down – no easy trick either. I prayed not to turn into a rolling stone gathering no moss.

The next day we visited Maligne Canyon, and started at the top of the canyon, hiking down a mile or so to see gorgeous waterfalls on the way, The descent was strenuous enough, but seeing the hikers' faces as they struggled back up told a horror story all its own. I haven't seen so much pain and suffering since the premier of *The World's Biggest Loser*.

Luckily, when we reached bottom, physically and emotionally, there was a parking lot and Larry volunteered to hike back up alone to get the car. Bless him. But then again, he was spared watching his friends exit the park on gurneys, escorted by Royal Mounties.

Perhaps saving the best for last, we headed to Lake Louise, where 19th Century Canadian Pacific Railroad barons built a spectacular hotel with the most stunning glacier-covered mountain views. Our week long fitness regimen paid off on our last long hike around the lake. Glorious.

Wow, I am so busy talking about outdoor activities I haven't mentioned food, which is really scary. We enjoyed fabulous salmon, trout, black cod, and halibut plus delicious bison burgers in many a rustically decorated restaurant. I passed on Elk stew.

By the way, we went through customs into Canada as family, as they honored our 2003 Vancouver wedding. Great feeling. Coming back to the U.S., not so much.

So here's the thing. I loved the trip. If a Jewish American Princess is hiking in the woods and there's nobody there to see her enjoy it, is she still a Jewish American Princess?

Next time, frickin' hiking poles. ▼

August 2009

I think I have overdosed on cuddly cute Schnauzers. All breeds, for that matter. It's been the year of the dog and it's only been a week.

Oddly, this has to do with golf. Many of my friends trotted off last week to an LPGA tournament in Chicago called the Solheim. From my theatrical point of reference I kept calling it the Sondheim which I think annoyed people.

But as Team Rehoboth left to watch the match, what to do with their four-legged sons and daughters? They all came to my house, Camp Schnauzerhaven.

We had our own two, Moxie and Paddy, plus Paddy's litter-mates Cody and Kelli, and another distant sibling, Ashley. Then it got weird. Niki the Yorkie checked in along with Gentle Ben the Airedale.

I know, seven. But with Bonnie as the resident Alpha dog, I'm just another pack member and that makes eight which is truly enough. Actually, on two different occasions last week we had day spa clients for grooming, so the thundering herd swelled yet again.

Each of the boarders checked in with their own food, treats, bedding, leashes, clean-up bags and toys.

Luckily, like me, most of the guests were of a certain age. Also like me, they were more interested in food than exercise. There are some amazing parallels here.

After check-in we had a meet and greet cocktail party featuring ice cold beverages and Snausages. Most of the shorter guests sampled from the bowls on the floor. Gentle Ben had happy hour in a raised porcelain bowl in another room. Ewwwww, yuk. As for me, I was the only one having Grey Goose on the rocks, and a lot of it.

Dinnertime. Each guest came on vacation with his or her own dietary regimen, requiring great coordination by staff to fill the bowls with the correct choices and have all entrees come out of the kitchen and onto the floor at the same time.

The chef had to juggle diners requesting yogurt on the side, green beans and carrots atop kibble, a variety of pills inserted in a variety of incentive choices and an assortment of measurements for portion control. With meals prepared, seating assignments (or would that be standing assignments?) needed to be made.

Bonnie and I mapped out the standing chart and starting calling names and placing bowls. Incredibly, each dog waiting until their name was called and then went obediently to where we pointed. Nobody tried to slip us a treat for a better table. I've seen rowdier crowds downtown waiting for tables.

Moxie! Paddy! Ashley! Niki! Cody! Kelli! Ben! Like clockwork.

The trouble began when the hoovers among them, namely my Moxie with Ashley a close second scarfed up their meals and went trolling for leftovers. Or didn't wait for leftovers and stood breathing down their prey's backs until they could make their move. There was a lot of snarling and whining and of course that was from me, as we humans got served last.

Then the pack needed to go out. Moxie! Paddy! Ashley! Niki! Cody! Kelli! Ben! Out they obediently trouped, most of them going off the deck for their evening constitutional.

One dog who shall remain nameless insisted on creating a literal poop deck.

Moxie! Paddy! Ashley! Niki! Cody! Kelli! Ben! Time to come in. We always had to count heads, and Kelli was always missing until we went out and carried her in personally. From that moment on she became Princess Grace Kelli.

After dinner came TV time and the flock took their positions on the living room floor, sofa or comfy laps. Amazingly peaceful – until a doorbell went off on a commercial and the whole house erupted.

But nighttime was my favorite. I've heard of three dog night, but this was ridiculous.

Four pack members insisted on sleeping in bed with Alpha: Niki, Ashley, Paddy and me. The rest took positions on the floor as IEDs (Improvised explosive devices) booby trapping my route to the bathroom.

And then came the storm. At the first huge crash of thunder Cody and Moxie also leapt on the bed. And they all started shaking and drooling in response to the thunder and lightning, turning our Posturepedic into one of those sleazy motel vibrating beds. And it continued for over an hour. Ben slept through it, the upside to hearing loss.

By morning the routine began anew. Moxie! Paddy! Ashley! Niki! Cody! Kelli! Ben! Time to go out, then breakfast. Then naps, then snacks, then playtime, then snacks, then naps, then dinner, then....

It was such a great routine I hated going off to work and missing it. So I quit my full-time job. Really. Honest. Done. I intend to be a stay-at-home pack member, writing this column, doing some freelance work and getting my napping skills just right.

Ashley went home on Saturday, then Cody and Kelli on Monday. Niki is checking out sometime tomorrow and Ben has a late check-out the next day.

Pretty soon it will be Alpha, me, Moxie and Paddy, alone again, naturally.

I'm looking forward to an afternoon snooze and some kibble, followed by a martini made by the leader of the pack. I know they say that unless you're the lead dog, the scenery never changes, but for now, I'm perfectly content to follow the fleet.

Did somebody say treats? I'm so there. A bath? I'm next in line. Flea dip? You can never be too careful. I'd like the rainbow collar please. I'll pass on the game of Frisbee, but I sure could use a nice walk.

Ahhhhh. Retirement. Sit/Stay. Pardon me if I go take a snooze. I'll try to keep my muddy paws off the furniture, but I can't promise.▼

September 2009

There's nothing like spending the day with old friends out on the water. Especially since it was in the best kind of boat – somebody else's.

As a former boat owner I can tell you that Bonnie and I spent 13 years boating on Chesapeake Bay and we have pitiful 401Ks to prove it. Boating is one expensive hobby.

So there I was, lounging on this boat, with no fiscal responsibilities, enjoying the water, the weather and the relaxation. Everyone aboard but me had a fishing pole and I can report that I caught as many fish as they did.

As we headed for a restaurant along an area called Kent Narrows I smiled, as this glorious September day reminded me of one from many years ago. Same captain, same crew.

Back then, our buds invited us boating "to run the gas down" so they wouldn't leave the boat with a full tank all winter. We gladly accepted the invite.

As we boarded the vessel, I said, "Let me go back to the car for my camera." I was as prolific back then with film as I am today with digital.

"The heck with it," said Bonnie, "for once, dammit, just go out and enjoy the ride without all the camera business."

Obviously, Bonnie was starting to view me as paparazzi, so I reluctantly agreed to leave the camera behind.

A half hour later, as we reached the middle of the Bay, near the famed Chesapeake Bay Bridge, I asked the captain how long it would take to run the gas down to an acceptable winter level. "I mean does it have to be empty on the gauge?"

"Well, said the captain, "the gauge is broken so it's hard to know, but we have plenty of gas, so let's just run around a while and head back."

At which point the boat's engine hiccupped, belched, bubbled, then quit.

Apparently we'd had a lot less gas than the broken gauge was able to indicate.

"Crap," said the first mate, "we're in the shipping channel.

Now, for my non-boating readers, simply put, being in the channel meant we'd likely wind up as flotsam and jetsam if a large boat came along. There's a lane in the middle of the wide bay, marked by buoys, that is deep enough for giant oil tankers and container ships filled with Mitsubishis. That's the channel. We were stalled in it, or at least perilously close to it and we'd all heard stories of small boats being hit and sunk by tankers, or perhaps even scarier, being sucked to the deep by the undertow of a passing cargo ship.

Of course, we instantly grabbed the marine radio to call for help. The sheepish captain's face said it all. "Um, the radio is supposed to go to the shop tomorrow. It only gets channel 17, so I hope somebody is listening." By this time Bonnie and I were incredulous as well as scared, and re-evaluating our relationship with boating and its boaters.

So we put out a call on the radio and waited for a reply. Nothing.

In the meantime, Bonnie tapped me on the shoulder, pointed toward the horizon and said, "What's that?"

In the distance, beyond the bridge, a boat approached. A very big boat.

"What is it, a tanker?" Bonnie asked.

"I dunno," said the captain."It's tall, and almost looks like a passenger ship."

"Is that Leo DiCaprio on the front? Damn, I see several smokestacks," I said, watching the enormous blob lumber toward us, slicing the water, heading for the bridge. The thing was so big, in fact, it looked like Pittsburgh on a barge and I doubted it would even fit under the bridge.

"Holy shit," or a version thereof, said everybody.

We held our breath as this behemoth gained on us. Exactly how much trouble were we in? From the look of things, the monster vessel was hugging the left side of the channel and we, in the equivalent of a rubber bathtub ducky were off right. Maybe, just maybe, we would luck out. But then again I didn't know the clearance required to avoid being sucked into the depths.

"My God, it's clearing the bridge by inches." I said, with the first mate adding "good thing the water's calm." Well, the water was the only one.

"Look at that thing!" "Holy Moly." "I'm peeing."

"Oh my God, it is a passenger ship. I've never seen so many decks in my life." I said, now looking up at an increasingly steep angle, with the giant bow approaching. Then, as we watched in dumbstruck awe, our eyes looked heavenward as the bow, with its massive anchor and chain, then the side, with its hundreds of staterooms and lifeboats, then the stern, pushed by its colossal propeller passed above us, regaling us with the giant lettering Queen Elizabeth II.

It was a passenger ship alright and when I realized, remarkably, that we were still afloat , I was incredibly pissed not to have a camera.

We watched the ocean liner's hind end travel down the bay, its wake causing us to bob up and down like that aforementioned bathtub toy and frantically called again for a tow.

Hooray! Somebody heard us on channel 17 and said, "I read you, changing to Channel 16."

"No!!!" we yelled, too late, understanding that the rescuer was being polite, getting off the open channel and telling us to go to channel 16 for a private conversation. Only we had no channel 16.

We tried again on our lone 17.

Our hero came back. "Switch to 16. Over and out." Click. God he had ants in his pants.

"Nooooo!" we hollered, despairing of getting his attention in time to get out of the channel before Moby Dick or The Titanic came by.

Finally, on the third try he listened long enough to understand our dilemma. We told him our location and he promised to be out to get us as fast as he could.

Meanwhile, the most beautiful sunset I have ever seen, before or since, took place on the Western shore of the bay, framing the departing QE II in a pink glow and providing us with the show of our lives.

No camera. My spouse knew there would be consequences.

Finally, the Lucky 5 rescue boat appeared to haul our lucky four asses back to shore.

In the ensuing years, and there have been many of them, that captain and first mate have remained two of our closest friends, fuel emergency and broken radio not withstanding. They've purchased a new boat and, for the record, have kept it in tiptop shape. We've boated with them often and somebody always makes a snide comment about running the gas out.

So here we were, almost two decades later, heading back to shore from our fabulous day on the water, when a stunning sunset appeared.

"Hey team," I said. "How 'bout a photo." So they dutifully posed on deck, before the lovely setting sun.

I was using the fancy 8-megapixel camera on my new Droid phone. But the battery had gone dead. No camera. Dammit. We all laughed.

What comes around, floats around. ▼

HEALTH INSURANCE ISN'T INSURANCE; IT'S PRE-PAID HEALTH CARE

Suppose that slimy Geico Gecko charged you, every year for your premium, the amount it would cost to buy a brand new car. Would that be car insurance? I think not.

Consider it in terms of this whole health insurance boondoggle and see why I have to go with my gut here.

My gut requires very little care and I can eat (and, of course, have happily eaten) pretty much anything without requiring a prescription medication. But because once, a millennium ago, I thought I was having a heart attack, which turned out to be gas, I am considered high risk for digestive issues and almost uninsurable.

Oddly, this was just academic for me a month ago. While I myself had employer paid insurance, I very much favored an expansion of Medicare as the new "public option" for those people not as fortunate as I.

How quickly things change. Now I am without any employer paid coverage and must venture into the mythical "open market" for *individual* health insurance. News flash! I cannot get any. That's right, as an individual I am totally uninsurable because I am fat and over 60. And I'm not even the 800 lb woman on *Discovery Health* every night.

Even people we consider to be trim and shapely are over the weight limit imposed by most insurers for individual coverage. I don't know about you, but I've earned my excess pounds with some pretty heavy carbohydrate loading. I'd hate to be working out like crazy and eating whole grains and *still* be considered too fat for insurance.

I may, however, be able to get insurance through my business, A&M Books, so here's what I found out. The problem is not health care; it's health insurance, a completely separate issue. And most people, along with politicians, pundits and pontificators are conveniently forgetting that fact.

There's nothing wrong with the health care I get. Love my doctor; happy with my choices of practitioners in the Rehoboth area. This dire crisis is *NOT* about doctors, end of life decisions, abortion, death panels, illegal aliens, deficits or all the other apple scrapple folks are trying to shove down our sore throats.

No, it's about access to affordable health insurance and unless you are a 27 year old Olympic athlete who's never even had a hangnail, insurance companies don't want any part of you. And if they do want a part, it's an organ that has never hiccupped. What organ would that be, our stiff upper lips?

Here's a dirty little secret. Insurance companies are no longer even selling health *insurance*, a product which involves a large enough pool so the risk of covering old sick people is outweighed by the reward of covering young healthy people. No, they are peddling pre-paid health *care*, an entirely different product. The paradigm shifted while we weren't looking.

Insurance companies no longer accept risk. They don't want no stinkin' risk. If you are 60 and fat and will need a colonoscopy and a flu shot in the next six months your premium will reflect exactly what they expect those things to cost.

My business has been quoted $900 a month for a policy for one employee, me, with a $5000 deductible. If I pay $900 a month for a year, plus my $5000 deductible, I am paying $15,800 (a year!) before the insurance company takes even the slightest risk. Meanwhile, they are raking in money from me and that healthy young buck requiring not so much as a tongue depressor.

I'm risking that my health care will cost more than a new Lexus, otherwise I'm just paying insurance company CEOs, lobbyists and favored candidates when I could just be paying the doctor or the hospital directly. This is insurance?

Okay, so you get this, right? If the insurance behemoths do want you, they want to make damn sure you pay them enough to actually fund all the MRIs, doctors visits, prescriptions and tests that a person your age will likely have. It's like pre-paying for your funeral – and under this system we are lucky if one doesn't turn into the other.

Now doubtless some folks will argue that my health care could cost more than $15,800 a year if I get really, really sick. But isn't that the kind of risk the insurance company should take in order to profit from some lucky jerk who pays money year after year and never so much as sneezes?

And how 'bout that lower-cost government option that tea-baggers, blow-hards, and legislators yelling "Liar!" think will turn us into a third world communist country? We all see that public education has killed private schools and universities. And Medicare put all the big insurance companies out of business, too. Puleeeze!

Tomorrow I have to call around for more health "insurance" quotes. I can picture it.

"Hello, you have reached Giveusyourwalletincorporated."

"Dial 1 if you are old and fat."

"Dial 2 if you have ever belched."

"Dial 3 if you were seen by a doctor coming out of the vaginal canal."

"Dial 4 if you think we paid off enough legislators to keep it business as usual."

Mel Brooks or Allan Sherman, or some funny guy wrote new lyrics to the song "Blue Skies" and called it "Blue Cross."

(sing it with me...)

Blue Cross,
said I would be
happy that
Blue Cross,
covered me.

Then I took a fall
leg in a splint

they said that I
should read the fine print.

And when a high
fever I ran
they said that I
bought the wrong plan.

Oh Blue Cross,
there seems to be
plenty for
Blue Cross
nothing for me.

Pray for Obama Care.▼

MARCH ON!

I hope some of my friends went to DC for the October 11 Equality March and marched for me.

When I heard about the October 11 national march I was terribly disappointed. Bonnie and I and the pups were in P-Town for Women's Week doing book signings and having a grand time. Who the heck scheduled the march on a day when thousands of East Coast lesbians would be heading for Cape Cod???

Dammit, I haven't missed a gay march on Washington since I came out of the closet in 1980.

For the first national march, in 1979, Bonnie was there in my place only she didn't know it. We hadn't met yet. In the midst of my coming out angst, I hungrily read all about the March but didn't have the guts to go.

1979 was the first nationwide march but it, like all marches following, was highly controversial. Maverick gay rights activists wanted to pressure Congress and the Carter White House; more conservative activists thought it would accomplish nothing but incite backlash. Both were right. Pressure was applied – a great deal, and very visible. But soon, like Anita Bryant getting a pie in the face, came the backlash.

The second national march was October 11, 1987. By then I was queer, I was here, I was not only used to it, but wondered what had taken me so long. Bonnie and I, in our late 30s had been together five years, parenting our first Schnauzer.

That day on the Mall, according to the *New York Times*, drew about a half a million people. It was the start of the great estimate wars between the Park Service, organizers and the media. It sure felt like a half a million marchers supporting gay rights and demanding action from the Reagan administration in the fight against AIDS. The event also included the first public display of Cleve Jones' NAMES Project AIDS Memorial Quilt.

It was a day of highs and lows: incredibly happy among my peers but remarkably sad to walk silently, under threatening skies, between panels of the quilt, stopping to, quite literally, read it and weep. How and why did this deadly epidemic target such bright, warm, loving people? And how dare the police on horseback guard us by wearing rubber gloves and sneering. Of course, the photographers snapped just the drag queens and dykes on bikes while the contingent of gay business people or PFLAG parents would never make the news.

Bonnie and I, quite amazingly, ran into Marge, a dear, long lost friend of Bonnie's in the half-million throng. We knew other friends were on the Mall, but with cell phones yet to be part of our consciousness, we couldn't find anybody.

By the April 25, 1993 National March a lot had changed and a lot hadn't. Organizers estimated 1,000,000 attended the March, but the National Park Service estimated attendance at (duh) 300,000. We lined up at the Washington Monument early in the morning. Our Maryland contingent didn't step off to march toward the White House until afternoon because locals (MD,VA & DC) go last. We missed all the speeches on the Mall since there were a million freakin' people ahead of us! I'm swearing by the organizers' count.

The '93 marchers were pissed at Bill Clinton and Don't Ask, Don't Tell, but we were also celebrating things like more religious organizations hosting same-sex commitment cere-monies, the possibility of marriage equality in Hawaii (that went down in flames!) and more and more public acceptance of gay relationships.

Again, LGBT (although I cannot remember whether T was added to the acronym by then or not) people poured out of the metro stations, restaurants, hotels and stores. Downtown Washington looked like a night at a dance club. Yes, there were demands for equality, yes, there was reverence and sadness for the people we lost, but yes, there was also tremendous optimism and slogans to make you laugh and cry. We marched chanting "Hey, Hey, Ho, Ho, Homophobia's got to go."

Again, Bonnie and I walked with our posse, minding our own business, when we drifted past the California contingent, and who do we run smack into – Marge from Norfolk. Go figure.

Fast forward to the new Millennium and the Equality 2000 March. Crowd estimators jockeyed between 200,000 and a million, and there were celebs galore with a sold out Equality Rocks concert the night before. My favorite posters were *Focus on your own damn family* and *Respect is not an agenda*.

We cheered Vermont's contingent and their new civil union law; college and high school groups, churches and synagogues, happy dads and cheering kids with the sign *Men With Strollers*, gay veterans and more. I think we cheered that we survived the Y2K scare.

The difference from prior marches? While there was still plenty of wonderful diversity, there was far less spectacle. Where once the Park Police wore riot gear and rubber gloves, this time they strolled their steeds through the crowds, chatting and visiting. And everybody and their grandmother had a cell phone.

We thought a lot about those who marched in '79, '87 or '93, and who were no longer with us, felled by AIDS or other deadly illnesses. We were getting older. In fact, our crew dropped in and out of the march several times, resting up on the sidelines. Still marching after all these years.

But we were there.

And we missed this one. I hope Marge was there. But since hey, hey, ho, ho, homophobia still has to go, I guess there will be another and these old dykes will get to march again. The more things change, the more they stay the same.

What do we want? Marriage Equality! When do we want it? NOW!▼

November 2009

Leaving 9-5 behind to be a full-time writer, it didn't take me long to utter the phrase I was told would eventually come out of my mouth: "I don't know how I had time to work."

Sadly though, I've spent most of my days answering the door and arguing on the phone. Very little writing is getting done.

Actually, part of my time has been spent working out in-house territory rights with Bonnie and the dogs, who are not used to having me underfoot all day.

I admit, I'd be a little ticked too if my spouse, who used to be absent all day, was suddenly home running her mouth. Bonnie frequently sends me to my room to write.

So I'm in the den trying to compose language and Moxie is pissed off that he is no longer allowed to bark indiscriminately at joggers. And apparently, Paddy used to spend his days curled up in front of the file cabinet I keep opening and he's ready to go for my throat. Now Bonnie is standing at the den door complaining that she's been on her hands and knees for two days installing laminate wood flooring and her hips and butt hurt. Frankly, the way this has been going, I'm pleased she has a pain in the ass that's not me.

Finally, we agreed to sign the Schnauzerhaven accords. They stay out of my way, I stay out of their way and we all come back together for dinner like usual.

That would be great if I could just write, but most of my work time has been spent on the phone, arguing with nincompoops like Expedia.com. All I wanted was a flight-hotel-car package for a weekend wedding in, of all places, Austin, Texas.

I got a flight for two, a cheap car (a Yugo?) and a room. Fine. I wouldn't even be in Austin long enough to see the million bats fly out from under that famous bridge at dusk. Given that Molly Ivins is dead, the bat thing was really the only reason, besides the wedding, ever to spend a dime to go to Texas.

Imagine my surprise when Expedia charged my Visa card for two vacation packages – a total of four people flying to Texas, two Yugo rentals and a pair of hotel rooms. Short of inviting two other people to Austin not to see the bats, this was redundant. I lodged a complaint with Visa.

Then I went to call Expedia Customer Service. Ever try to find a phone number for a dotcom? Expedia doesn't want to talk to its customers so badly they hide the phone number like Where's Waldo. Oh, here it is in 2-point type.

For new reservations push one, for existing reservations push two, for vacation packages push three, for anxiety medication push four....

"All vacation specialists are helping other customers right now and...."

Vacation specialists? *I'm* a vacation specialist. These people are aggravation specialists. On hold, I put down the land line.

Then I made a cell phone call. Medicare had approved a new power wheelchair for my dad months ago and the government had already paid the supply company. Despite six months of calls to a woman named Christine, the chair has not been delivered. Dad is 91. You'd think they'd see some reason for expedia. Dot com.

So I called Medicare. A phone robot said "For Medicare selections say 'one,' for Part B say 'two,' for all other questions say 'other.'

"Other."

"I'm sorry," said the robo-answerer, "I didn't get that, can you repeat?"

Of course I can repeat but how can I say "other" any clearer? I wasn't gargling the first time.

"O-T-H-E-R."

"You have reached the Medicare Customer Service line. All operators are busy assisting other customers..."

Now there are two phones on hold in speaker mode with dueling elevator music.

Trapped at my desk, I played video games. Finally, the Expedia operator picked up. I described my dilemma.

"Yes," she said, "on reservation 288 we have Fay and Bonnie leaving from Philadelphia in seats 17A & B, changing in Atlanta to seats 21A & B and arriving in Austin. We also have reservation 291 for Fay and Bonnie leaving from Philadelphia in seats 11A & B, changing in Atlanta to seats 14 A & B and arriving in Austin. Is that correct?

"No, that's not correct. Don't you see a problem with this?" I asked.

"You have paid for two packages," she said.

"Yes, but the two of us cannot take up four airplane seats that are not adjacent to each other no matter how porky we are. Hell, if the seats were contiguous we could use the elbow room, but as it stands this is just wrong."

She did not have a sense of humor. She said she'd check into it and call me back.

By this time Medicare took me off hold and I explained that the new chair had not been delivered, the current chair had both wheels leaning north, sending Dad in circles, which was what the wheelchair supply company was doing to us.

I have to say, the Medicare (government option!) people got right on it, checking the records and transferring me to the fraud division. I hope the chair people have good lawyers.

Okay, back to writing. But then the doorbell rings, setting the dogs off. Some teenager wants to re-seal my driveway. No thanks.

Barnum and Bailey had just calmed down when the doorbell rings again, with a hapless salesman trying to sell me a frozen side of beef. "Sorry, eating light these days!"

Then Expedia comes back on the line telling me they are e-mailing me a letter to sign and fax back immediately, swearing I will call off the Visa investigation until they sort it all out. Failure to do so would cancel both packages and keep me from going to Texas not to see the bats.

I considered it.

away for deeply closeted singles and couples to enjoy themselves in relative anonymity. "Although we weren't called gay then. We were still homosexuals," jokes one Rehoboth old-timer.

He and his cronies recall a very cultured, sophisticated gay scene. Hundreds of gay men would gather at what became known as Carpenter Beach in front of the du Pont mansion to relax on the sand, set up chess and backgammon boards and play volleyball.

UNDER THE RADAR

From the 1950s through the early '70s, the gay scene moved exclusively between beach and private house parties, since there were no specifically anointed gay bars. Even if there was a welcoming bar, liquor laws at the time prevented anyone, gay or straight from walking around carrying a drink. Under those circumstances, even if gays gathered at a gay tolerant establishment "it was almost impossible to meet anyone other than the fellow sitting right beside you" recalls one patron of the former Pink Pony bar on the boardwalk, where The Boardwalk Plaza now stands.

While it catered to a predominantly heterosexual crowd, gay men frequented the early evening happy hour. While not gay himself, owner Jim Booth is remembered as gay-friendly and happy to have had this new clientele. Up the block, The Pleasant Inn, at Olive Avenue and First Street, and several other guest houses, had a word-of-mouth reputation as gay-friendly as well.

With the ever present threat of exposure that could lead to loss of employment, or even imprisonment, most of these vacationing men kept strictly to their area of the beach and partied mostly at their closest friends' homes. Each weekend, small dinner parties, many formal and elegant, took place at numerous antique filled homes around Rehoboth Beach. It was a very discreet, very chic gay crowd.

This underground society communicated quite clandes-tinely in Washington, D.C., during the week, arranging parties and overnight guest accommodations. When the men, along with an increasing number of lesbians, came to Rehoboth for the weekends, they could gather in an atmosphere relatively free from threats of exposure or physical danger.

One lesbian couple, Anyda Marchant and Muriel Crawford, lived on Laurel Street in Rehoboth. "As far as we knew for sure, in the 60s and 70s we were the only ones," Anyda recalled in 2005, just before her death at age 95. She and Muriel, would take long walks around their neighborhood and every now and then they would spot a man or woman they thought might be gay as well. "We said, 'Look, there's a shush.' We couldn't even say the word homosexual."

While The Pink Pony was destroyed by the great 1962 nor'easter, the Nomad Village, a motel, bar and package store which opened in 1960 just south of the Indian River Inlet, survived the storm. According to former Nomad employee Jim Short, Randall Godwin and his wife, Betty, opened the Nomad with no thought that it would become a huge part of Rehoboth-area gay history.

"I didn't start out to have a gay bar, but it just sort of happened," Randall Godwin said in an interview more than a decade ago. He said he opened a separate room for gays because he was afraid there would be fights with the straight bar patrons if he didn't.

"It's generally accepted that straights think I caused what was then called 'the gay problem' in the area," Godwin said. "But it's not true. They were already coming here from Washington, D.C." Because traditional families weren't supporting Nomad Village the way he envisioned, "economically it just made sense to cater to the gays," Godwin said.

Word spread that the Nomad back room was a great meeting spot for closeted folks from D.C. and, increasingly from Philadelphia and Baltimore, too. In the years right after the 1969 Stonewall riots for gay rights in New York City, the bar's popularity surged.

Rehoboth resident Fran Hueber and his late partner, Ross

Alexander, met at Carpenter Beach in the late 1960s and frequented the Nomad. "It was a very low-key sort of gay society here," Hueber recalls. Alexander opened one of the first gay-owned retail businesses in town: Joss, an upscale gift shop at the corner of Baltimore Avenue and First Street, where a furniture store now stands. When Alexander died in 2002, the couple had been together for 37 years.

Many folks who went to the Nomad in the '60s and '70s remember being asked their names and having to sign in. Godwin insisted that this was not harassment – rather, he was just trying to keep the place a private club so he wouldn't be harassed. "We charged $5 to join and then a $3 cover with three tickets given out – good for three beers or two drinks."

THE DISCO ERA

From 1972 though the 1980s, the Godwins fought the county over Nomad Village's zoning designation. And more than once they heard tales that lawmakers and county officials were "not going to do anything to keep that queer joint open," he recalled. But open it stayed, and by the mid-'80s it was catering to an increasing number of lesbians visiting Sussex County as well.

Throughout those years, Rehoboth's reputation as a traditional family resort continued to build, while at the same time, more gay visitors arrived. Two gay dance clubs, the Boathouse and the Renegade, opened to celebrate the disco era, and 300 to 400 gay men could generally be found on the beach at the south end of the Rehoboth boardwalk on most weekends. The numbers swelled on summer holiday weekends.

On July 4, 1973, the Boathouse, opened by Francis Murphy, a Wilmington gay bar owner, and a straight couple, Sid and June Sennebaum, premiered at the water's edge in Dewey Beach. Wanting to ensure that the former Hawaiian-themed bar turned gay establishment would be a success, and free of harassment, Murphy hatched a unique business plan. He'd hire football players from the University of Delaware as bouncers. But he had rules. In exchange for their promise never to utter one syllable of anti-gay talk – on or off the job – and to be fully supportive of the operation and its patrons, Murphy agreed to pay them $75 a night, which was double what other bar owners paid. As an added incentive, their girlfriends were welcome at the bar and could have free drinks. But one breach of the rules and they would be out without their fat paychecks. It was a winning contract.

The Boathouse was a spacious room, with a long bar at one side, and a big dance floor at the front. At high tide on the bay, water sometimes crept up to the porch, which was out over the water. Former patron David Leigey remembers that more than once customers helped sweep out the tidal waters from the brick floor.

With a clientele of 70 percent men, and 30 percent women, the place was generally packed with area visitors and the increasing number of gay men and women settling in coastal Sussex.

Former patrons tell amazing tales about the Boathouse. In addition to the hundreds of gays vacationing in Rehoboth and coming to the Boathouse, the club attracted FBI and CIA agents, U.S. senators, and members of the Washington Redskins. People came to Rehoboth just to go to the Boathouse.

Longtime couple Lee Mills and Don Gardiner, who now have a home and business in Rehoboth, remember a visit here in the summer of 1975. "The stretch between Ocean City and Dewey was a barren wasteland except for the Nomad – which is where we heard about The Boathouse. We drove to Dewey, turned off Route One and just followed the stream of boys heading toward the water from all directions.

"The place was really jumping. It was magical – even though it was in town, it was like a desert oasis," Mills recalls.

But the good times lasted only a few years, until the Boathouse burned down. Was it intentional – a hate crime before that phrase was even made into a law? There are suspicions but no answers.

In May 1980, the Renegade dance club, owned by Glen Thompson, a D.C. bar operator, opened on Route 1 just outside Rehoboth. Condos and a carwash now occupy the site.

Busy from the first night, the Renegade was a smash. But less than eight weeks later, on July 4, 1980, the place burned to the ground in the middle of the night. Was that a hate crime? Thompson doesn't think so. "We really had no trouble with the local people."

Whatever the fire's origin, it devastated the business and the summer crowd. Determined to rebuild, Thompson worked closely with Sussex County officials, who did everything possible to help the Renegade get its permits to reopen by Labor Day, Thompson recalls.

By a conservative estimate, 30,000 people dined, danced, saw shows, and in later years sang karaoke at the Renegade each year. It was also a custom for clubgoers to wind up at the Robin Hood Restaurant on Rehoboth Avenue for late-night breakfasts.

"Rehoboth was an integral part of my coming out," says Eastern Shore native and former Rehoboth resident Jon Mumford. "It was magical because it was the only place I knew there to be other gay people. I remember crazy nights at the Renegade."

While the early years saw the Renegade hosting many more men than women, by the mid-'80s, when the dance floor filled for the disco tune "It's Raining Men" there were lots of women there, too.

Rehoboth resident Julie Peters remembers good times at the Renegade. "It was really the only place to go to dance and it was always packed."

THE MOON RISES

The late '70s and early '80s hold special significance for Rehoboth's gay community because it was the dawn of Rehoboth Beach as a culinary destination. Within a couple of years of each other both the Back Porch and the Blue Moon restaurants opened. The Back Porch came first, opening in 1974 under owner Victor Pisapia and partners. Then, a few years later, Pisapia teamed up with Joyce Felton, a former New Yorker who worked at the Back Porch, to open the Blue Moon. It began a partnership that would dramatically alter the resort dining and gay nightlife scene.

On the weekend before Memorial Day 1981, with the polyurethane floors still drying and the liquor board due any second to check the place out, Pisapia and Felton opened the doors. And the Moon was mobbed.

The restaurant took off that first summer, as Pisapia and Felton concentrated on establishing a dinner crowd and staying open on weekends until 4 a.m. to catch patrons coming back from the Renegade.

As the Blue Moon received excellent notices from food critics at the *New York Times* and *Gourmet* magazine, the establishment got a different kind of notice from some folks in Rehoboth. For all the people delighted to have this upscale, urbane restaurant in town, there were others, very vocal, who were not happy at all.

Sometime during the first summer of operation, Rehoboth Mayor John Hughes, who has since completely changed his negative feelings about Rehoboth's gay population, called Pisapia and Felton into his office. It seems that somebody sent the mayor an article describing what he called "gay food in Rehoboth." Pisapia, who was closeted at the time, stayed very quiet. Joyce, on the other hand, wanted to know just exactly what made food gay.

"It's your clientele," came the answer. The mayor explained that there was no way this town wanted a gay restaurant. It was a warning.

While Pisapia and Felton worked seven days a week to keep the restaurant going, a mobilization began in town. There were meetings, sides were drawn and, as Felton recalls, rumors of an organization called AGVO – anti-gay vigilante organization. Just as Pisapia and Felton were frightened by the reactions the Blue

Moon unleashed, so too were the members of the opposition frightened by this new community they feared and didn't understand.

Amid the controversy, the Blue Moon continued to attract its diverse crowd and diverse reactions. It wasn't unusual for the restaurant to be pelted with tomatoes or beer cans from passing cars, just as it wasn't unusual for the dining room to be filled with both gay and straight diners, local business people and politicians.

According to Felton, on the night then-Governor.Mike Castle was having dinner at the Blue Moon, a full 16-ounce can of beer was hurled through the window just moments after his party departed. Fortunately, no one in the dining room was hurt – physically.

Things really heated up when the Blue Moon's neighbors got into the act, calling the City to complain about the bar and its clientele. If the police backed off and took a less aggressive stand about complaints, obsessive phone calls against the eatery forced them right back into the middle. Complaining neighbors and anti-gay residents had an agenda and the police were bound to investigate every call.

The harassment and threats continued for years.

But the customers kept coming. All kinds of customers. In addition to the loyal regulars, gay and straight, who savored the Blue Moon for its sophisticated food and ambiance, high profile customers like Frank Perdue, Baltimore Oriole Jim Palmer, Congressman Barney Frank, and Govovernor. Tom Carper dined at the Moon.

"The crowds didn't care about social unrest. They kept us in business," says Felton. "We just kept going."

In 1988, a disco named The Strand, backed by a group of Rehoboth business owners, including Felton, opened in the center of Rehoboth Beach, turning a shuttered movie house into a hot nightspot. Two years later, Steve Elkins, who had worked at the White House for President Jimmy Carter, and then in computer sales, was asked by his friend Joyce Felton to move to Rehoboth to manage the BYOB club. Elkins and his partner, Murray Archibald, an artist, traded their decade long weekend life in Rehoboth to move to the resort full time.

Under their watch, up to 700 bodies could be found dancing under disco glitter balls long into the night. The party was grand. But when the Strand continued to apply for a liquor license, the Rehoboth Homeowner's Association and other residents drew their line in the sand. "There was a petition passed around citing noise, traffic and parking concerns to bolster their pleas for denial," Elkins recalls, "but they got people to sign it by asking 'Do you want a gay club in your backyard?'

Other downtown businesses, afraid of losing their own rights came off the sidelines to support the Strand, but it was too late. The homeowners won. In 1995, the city voted to ban bars altogether, permitting only establishments that served food to hold liquor licenses. Today, the ordinance still states, "No person shall sell, give, dispense, provide or keep or cause to be sold, given, dispensed, provided or kept any alcoholic beverage on the premises of any dance hall establishment."

Several weeks after the vote, state troopers raided the Strand in a drug bust, arresting six people. Sadly for all its fans, the Strand could not survive the lack of a liquor license as well as the growing anti-gay sentiment in town. The Strand danced on for a while, but filed for bankruptcy protection in 1993, and, according to Steve Elkins, closed the next year.

CAMP REHOBOTH IS BORN

More trouble brewed. With gays and lesbians being much more visible in town by the early 1990s, many longtime residents feared their town was being overtaken by these newcomers. Bumper stickers appeared saying "Keep Rehoboth a Family Town" – which the gay community interpreted as anti-gay – and there were some violent gay-bashing incidents and less serious but equally upsetting instances of name-calling and harrassment.

Ron Tipton, now retired to the area from Philadelphia remembers being on Poodle Beach when "young toughs would occasionally stop by and threaten us."

It was then, in 1991, Murray Archibald, Steve Elkins and their friends in the business community thought about forming an organization to promote understanding between the gay the straight communities.

While more and more gays and lesbians headed for Rehoboth on summer weekends, drawn by the beautiful resort and the growing number of gay-friendly businesses, something needed to be done to bring the gay and straight communities together – and keep gay citizens safe.

According to Elkins, a frightening incident happened on the Boardwalk in 1992 when a man was attacked with a broken off champagne bottle and very seriously injured. A group of five teens – one old enough to be tried as an adult – was arrested and convicted, with the adult sentenced to five years in jail.

"Sadly," says Elkins," City officials did not want to make a statement about the incident. "They wanted to brush it under the rug." However, Elkins says, Rehoboth Police Chief Creig Doyle insisted it become public and Elkins was interviewed by the newspapers and WHYY-TV. One City Commissioner, Roger Poole, contacted Elkins the next day and thanked him. "I knew we had to reach out and let people know this was not accept-able," Poole remembers.

So, the organization CAMP Rehoboth was born, with CAMP being an acronym for Create A More Positive Rehoboth, along with a nod to the gay community's hallmark campiness. Since one of the interpretations of the Biblical word "Rehoboth" is "room for all," the name CAMP Rehoboth was a natural.

This fledgling nonprofit organization of gay volunteers (along with some straight allies) hosted meetings with local government, conducted sensitivity training with the police department and met with homeowner associations to try to bring the diverse communities closer.

CAMP Rehoboth started with a four page newsletter, a small board of directors with Archibald as president, and a tiny office space in the courtyard at 39 Baltimore Avenue, just down the street from the Blue Moon.

Along with its mission of bringing the communities together, the gay community itself needed a hub. While there were a growing number of places to dine and dance, with an increasing number of welcoming B&Bs, restaurants and shops, there was no central focus – a place people could come for information about the community. And it wouldn't hurt to have a way of reaching out for understanding and cooperation between members of the gay and lesbian community and the local merchants, government, year-round and summer residents, and anyone else calling Rehoboth home.

"Our goal was to work with the entire community," says Elkins, currently executive director of the organization. "After all, if we were isolated, with divisions in the community, we wouldn't really be a living representation of what the rainbow symbol, long associated with the gay community, means."

MAKING PROGRESS

The organization, in addition to providing events and programs for the gay community, reached out to fight discrimination by promoting political awareness and developing relationships with the local media, police, government, community and clergy.

As time passed, CAMP Rehoboth, its volunteers and small staff became well-known in the community, assisting other non-profits, like the library with its book sales, the Independant Film Festival with volunteers or Beebe Hospital with its fundraising benefits. As local homeowners got to know these volunteers personally, the division between gay and straight residents started to narrow.

In May 2003, a sexual orientation anti-discrimination law was passed unanimously by the mayor and commissioners of Rehoboth Beach.

And since its formation in 1991, CAMP Rehoboth has seen incredible growth.

That four page newsletter has been known to go over 120 pages now, and instead of being available at a handful of sites, the magazine is delivered to Rehoboth area businesses, and many more in Washington, D.C., New York City, Philadelphia and Baltimore.

Gay life changed, as well. With more acceptance and visibility, people had more options for places to meet and spend time. As was the trend nationally, big dance clubs had trouble sustaining business other than on weekends. The Renegade, which closed its doors in 2003, gave way to smaller venues, mixing dining and dancing, and a gay community that was out and visible in the entire community.

On May 30, 2009, 19 years after its inception, CAMP Rehoboth held the grand opening for the new wing of its community center on Baltimore Avenue. The tiny starter space has grown into two adjacent in-town properties that house the CAMP Rehoboth office, a beautiful new room for events and meetings, a lending library and public computer access, as well as a home for businesses which rent space around the center courtyard.

The crowd at the grand opening included city commissioners, local business owners, politicians, bankers, and hundreds of CAMP Rehoboth supporters – gay and straight.

In another milestone, the signing of the bill that added the words "sexual orientation" to Delaware's nondiscrimination law took place July 2, 2009 at CAMP Rehoboth, with Governor Jack Markell and several legislators who had worked for passage of the bill in attendance.

Former Commissioner Roger Poole sees a big difference over the years. He and his wife Joyce are best friends with their gay neighbors and enjoy all the diversity the town offers. Roger was delighted to find his photo in a recent edition of *Letters from CAMP Rehoboth*. "Today I think that almost all of the residents here are comfortable sharing our town with the gay community."

Is life perfect, with discrimination entirely gone? Of course not. But it is infrequent and only whispered to like-minded individuals. "They are missing out on good friends," says Poole.

Today, Rehoboth Beach and the surrounding areas are home to a large gay population, many businesses owned and operated by gays and lesbians and a throng of gay visitors seamlessly blending with the community at large.

Joyce Felton finds the difference in the last quarter century amazing. "I'm truly grateful to have had the opportunity to live in a time and place to help make change – even if it was challenging and traumatic at times. My life has been enriched for it."

One example of how Rehoboth has evolved as a place with "room for all": In 2008, as *USA Today* called the resort one of America's best gay beaches, *Reader's Digest* anointed it one of America's top retirement destinations.

Part-time resident Peter Rosenstein has been visiting Rehoboth for many years and sees a huge difference today, from the 1980s. "It's the freedom today to be yourself and not be afraid of what others will think, it's the openness of the gay community and the feeling that Rehoboth is now one big community and not two separate ones."

As Steve Elkins is fond of saying, recalling that old bumper sticker, "Rehoboth is still a family town – for all kinds of families."▼

January 2010

Disney on New Year's Eve. What was I thinking?????

For the first time in a decade, my mate and I ventured outside Reho for the holidays. Given our current economic diet we simply could not pass up an invitation to spend a week with good friends in sunny Florida.

Alas, we actually had to get there, which required cramming the car with two suitcases, two overnight bags, two sets of golf clubs, two Schnauzers, and two winter-weary humans. Is there an uglier, more boring route that I-95? Our favorite roadside attractions included pictures of bloody fetuses on anti-abortion signs and a huge billboard erected by some pissed off people warning "Waldo, FL Speed trap!" The Chamber of Commerce must be pleased. Sure enough, there was a black and white with sirens atop lying in wait. Thank you, billboard people.

Lots of us have navigation systems now and it was eerily obvious when we hit a traffic snarl. Dozens of cars, us included, peeled off like lemmings through suspect neighborhoods at the insistence of, as we call her, the bitch on the dashboard. We blindly followed the pack until we came out the other side of the back-up. But frankly, she could have led us to the Amityville Horror House for all we knew. Does anyone else think this blind obedience is a little spooky?

Ah, the gourmet food choices en route. My favorite is Sonny's Barbecue, which, if I recall, was the last place I ever entered with an intact gall bladder. Sometime in the mid 1990s, returning from the South, I ate an enormous lard-laden dinner at a Sonny's and several miles down the road my gall bladder became an improvised explosive device.

As I moaned in pain, Bonnie said "I have to get you to a hospital!"

"Not in South Carolina you don't!"

So we drove non-stop, nine hours back to civilization so I

could have surgery where we might be treated as a legitimate couple.

But this time, filled with plenty of gall, but gall-bladderless, we stopped at Sonny's, with nothing left to lose. Just dignity. It was unwise eating all those baked beans and getting right back into the car. Turnabout is fair play: the Schnauzers sat in the back fanning the air.

But after a mere 19 hours of mindless driving we reached our destination.

Good friends, good food, good god they took me fishing. There's a reason there's no book called *Shoes of the Jewish Fisherman*. There I was, standing in the sun, waving my fishing pole, feeling my skin prematurely aging, with nothing on the hook to show for it.

Of course, the three other fisherpersons snagged trout, flounder and holy mackerel at an alarming pace, making me look like a slacker. Suddenly I felt a big tug at my line and managed to stutter "FFFish!"

"And she's a communication professional," said my spouse.

The captain grabbed my line, relieved me of a large silver trout and re-baited my hook. I've gotten lots of rebates in my time but this was my first rebait. "Fish!" I yelled, the process repeating itself. Within seconds of my line landing back in the water, I shouted "Fish!" again. In all, sixteen times.

When the sun set we pulled pants over our shorts, zipped up our jackets and shivered, speeding to shore with our haul. While the three amigos huddled in morbid fascination as the captain gutted the fish, I sat in the car with the butt warmer on. If I wanted to see that many entrails I could just as easily watch *Life in the ER* on Discovery.

We ate our trophy fish that night, then spent a day or two playing golf and looking at alligators. Simultaneously. It's impossible to concentrate on your tee shot when a nine-foot alligator with bulging eyeballs is staring you down from twenty feet away. My game suffered, but I still have all my body parts.

Golf, fishing, sun, fun behind us, we headed home – with

a last stop, on New Year's Eve in Disney World. I did love it, but two things are clear. First, Disney is the only place I can spend more money per minute than in a casino. Second, nowhere in my entire life, including Times Square, have I ever been crammed amid more teeming humanity, pushing and shoving toward a good time. But it was Disney, so as crowded as it was, there was no actual rioting. At one point even Mickey got testy.

In the Magic Kingdom we made the mistake of going on a spaceship ride in Tomorrowland which was made for our bodies from yesteryearland. We climbed into the minuscule airplane, wedging ourselves into the fuselage like a stepmother's clodhopper in a glass slipper.

"Good heavens, are we going to be able to get out of this thing?" I asked as it rocketed upward.

"Whamfth? said Bon, teeth lodged in my hoodie.

We had a spectacular view of the whole park from up there but spent most of the ride panicked we'd need Goofy and the fire brigade to get us out. We eventually dug our thighs free but not without synchronized screaming.

"Hey, maybe that oldie-but-goodie It's a Small World ride will be more hospitable." I said. Frankly, we were surprised to find they'd spent significant money to make the boats smaller, lower and considerably harder to get into since our last visit. Alas, it was a small ride after all.

But counting down to 2010 in Epcot was the biggest hoot. We downed champagne in every "country" in the park, watched a million bucks of fireworks usher in the new year and then tried to leave.

Ha! In a champagne stupor, we swept along with the mass exodus to the parking lots. No problem; nobody was going anywhere. Amid a symphony of beeping as owners pressed their keys, hoping to find their cars, we just put the seats back in our vehicle and slept it off. Happily, the dogs were bunking with Pluto at Epcot kennel.

It is not true that when you wish upon a star, anything your heart desires will come to you. My heart desired to be beamed up on January 1 and dropped back in Rehoboth, skipping the Waldo speed trap, Sonny's beans, Right-to-Life billboards, a thousand Cracker Barrels, and all of I-95.

M-I-C, see ya real soon, K-E-Y why? Because next time we fly in a wide-bodied jet. ▼

February 2010

For Rehoboth Beach, not used to wintery wallops, the snow removal policy is pretty much "the lord giveth, the lord taketh away."

Oh the weather outside WAS frightful on Super Bowl weekend 2010 and it caught lots of coastal residents by surprise. We hadn't seen so much snow here since 1996.

The citizenry gulped Thursday night February 4 when weather forecasters uttered the B-word, for blizzard. Pink blobs on the weather map warned of heavy snow for D.C., Baltimore and Philadelphia. Oddly, there was a bright orange blob, something reminiscent of Sigourney Weaver's *Alien* over Southern Delaware and New Jersey – preparing us to bear the brunt of the storm. Who are they kidding? We never get as much as they predict.

Friday late afternoon saw flurries, as brave souls made it along the messy roads to local watering holes for what might have been a last taste of restaurant food and bartender-fixed adult beverages. While we downed Cosmos, the flurries turned furious. Then came the Governor's announcement of a state-wide snow emergency with non-essential travel prohibited. I tried to determine if getting to Happy Hour had been essential. Yes.

It may well have been a state of emergency for folks who had neglected to get to the grocery, which, from the look of the ravaged shelves were damn few. It looked like a bomb had gone off in the toilet paper aisle.

So we were home by 9 p.m. on Friday, hunkered down with the pups and ready to sneer at forecasters for blowing things out of proportion once again.

Okay, it was big. We awoke Saturday to almost a foot of snow, backyard barbecue and patio furniture buried in dunes, white stuff still falling but with hopes it was tapering off.

Okay, it got bigger. Mea Culpa to the forecasters. Tree tops glistened and children listened to the entire neighborhood of shovelers grunting. As the dogs and I watched our Alpha clear the front walk, the path behind her filled up a fast as she shoveled. After only 15 minutes I was mate to the abominable snowman. Pretty soon the Yeti gave up and came inside.

The only thing happening faster than the snow was our consumption of empty calories. Why does being snowbound trigger our inner oinkers? The four of us huddled on the sofa, carbohydrate loading (dog biscuits are carbs, too) and ogling L Word reruns.

In fairness, I balanced my pathetic gulping with my new health food regimen: red wine and dark chocolate. They have been declared good for you. That's my story and I'm sticking to it.

By mid-day Saturday, hoping the snow was tapering off and thinking it might be safe to go back in the water…ing hole, the reverse happened. We got another dump, with major drifting from increased winds. Not only could we lose a Schnauzer in the drifts, but I was concerned about the BMW. Whiteout conditions ensued and we couldn't see two feet in front of our faces, much less where eight paws might search in vain for a spot of grass in the drift-contoured back yard.

When we opened the sunroom's sliding glass door to toss the two unsuspecting Schnauzers into the snow, concerns for their health, not to mention our carpets, were assuaged when we spied small areas of yellow snow. Good boys. Unfortunately, drifting snow blew into the door track, and unbeknownst to us kept the door from closing all the way. Next time we looked we had a bunny slope in the sunroom.

By late afternoon lights and cable flickered, frightening us into locating our K-Mart wind-up radio. Losing internet, TV, phone and lights, channeling Mary Todd Lincoln for Super Bowl weekend, was not my idea of a gay old time.

Fortunately or unfortunately the lights held, so we could see just how much popcorn and pizza we ate. Somebody stop me! That the cable survived was good too, because it was fun watching our local TV personalities, frostbit and turning into frozen margaritas, reporting live from the scene.

Come a sunny Sunday morning, the full extent of the mess revealed itself. Entire communities stood stranded by unplowed streets. The only action outside my house was the occasional groan from hikers struggling toward the re-opening grocery stores. Cigarettes ? Booze? Both? I wondered how long I'd last before setting out once we downed the last of the Chubby Hubby ice cream.

Some hardy and fool-hardy people started digging themselves out of the two-foot deluge. My mate and I took turns trying to free up one car and a path for it to back into the street. With both of us being middle aged (provided we live until 120) we were acutely aware of being cautious. One of us would do a 15-minute stint with our only snow shovel while the other would nag "bend your knees, don't lift too much at once, stop if you get winded," then we'd switch places and continue the nag-a-thon.

At one point an ambulance slogged up the road. We never saw it come back, since we instantly abandoned shoveling, thoughts of heart attacks and strokes dancing in our heads. After a few minutes inside with a *Law & Order* marathon and doctored hot chocolate, we determined we were not in acute medical danger but gave up shoveling anyway. If our street got plowed, Mt. Kilimanjaro would just get shoved onto our newly cleared driveway. So like Scarlet says in *Gone with the Wind*, "After all, tomorrow is another day."

And speaking of another day, by 1 p.m. Sunday the school board called off classes for both Monday and Tuesday. Some restaurants announced they would still fry chicken wings and serve beverages for the Super Bowl, but others threw in the towel and stayed dark. A quick check revealed it was the LGBT places keeping the lights on. We are a hardy lot.

With cameras snapping snowy sights, and kitchens all over the coast preparing football food, a blizzard covered Sussex

County took it in stride. While some folks dug out, others dug in for the big game. It sure looked toasty in Miami and New Orleans.

By Monday afternoon, after the Saints had come marching in to the goalposts, some neighborhoods were still cut off from civilization. Front end loaders had created mountains of dirty white ice and snow in medians, parking lots and throughout downtown Rehoboth. At traffic lights, most right turn lanes were blocked by great walls of snow, making turning an extreme sport. According to that Pennsylvania rodent Punxsutawney Phil, spring thaw is still six weeks away and from the look of things, the snow piles could last until June Pride Week.

On Tuesday morning it was starting to seem like the classic film *Groundhog Day*, with everything repeating itself. The weather forecast called for Snowmeggedon part two. Just a mere 8-10 inches this time. Mere.

Damn those necessities! We had plenty of toilet paper and milk, but dog food and mac 'n cheese were running low. My spouse, eager to play with her four-wheel drive vehicle, fought her way out onto the unplowed street, pioneering a path to the store. Yee-Ha!

Like a triumphant Lewis & Clark, we returned in time to hear the superintendant close school for the rest of the week. At this point Bonnie will be working until July 4th.

They say our climate change problems can cause violent weather shifts along with the disturbing rise in global temperatures. A little of that global warming would feel pretty good right about now. It might stop me from making the Rice Crispy treats...naaah.... Oh the weather outside is frightful but the snacks are so delightful, let it snow,, let it snow, let it...somebody stop me before I eat again....▼

March 2010

Sally Field can drink Boniva to strengthen her bones but I'm drinking beer.

It's been a weird winter alright, and just one of the strange things to come out of it was a University of California study revealing that beer is a rich source of something called silicon (as opposed to silicone for the boobs) which increases bone density and helps prevent osteoporosis. Hand me a Yuengling.

So I'm guzzling my health drink and marveling at the creative ways we managed to survive this terrible, terrible winter. Not that the Snowpocalypse didn't take its toll. Around Rehoboth, we were house bound so many days even the dogs got sick of lying on the sofa. They say killer whales get stir crazy in captivity, but they have nothing on me. The snow was as high as an elephant's eye, yet I was willing to risk a triple lutz in the street to get to Cloud 9 for a martini; I was eager to chance the driveway luge track to fight for my right to toilet paper at Food Lion; my god, I was even anxious to scoop pup poop in the back yard, only it was covered by 28 inches of snow.

"It's 14 degrees out. You're staying put," said my spouse. "Let's do Wii Fit training. "

I don't know if you are aware of this sadistic gym video or not, but you turn on the TV, put the disk into the machine and stand on a wireless plastic platform to get weighed. Within seconds a snarky cartoon character tells you your weight and body mass index. Like I wanted to know. What's worse, the little animation then says, out loud, in a judgmental voice, "You're obese."

What do you say to that? Stunned, I muttered "Gee, thanks. Are you aware I've already lost 25 pounds since summer?" Apparently not. According to Wii Fit, we (the Royal We) are not fit.

Furthermore, after a couple of balance and aerobic tests

the blasted cartoon informs me that my fit age is 65, which would be fine if I was 85. It would also be fine if I could get Medicare. But noooo, there is no justice. Having a computer-generated nudnick tell you your body is four years older than your actual age is highly mortifying. Not only am I stir crazy like Orca, I weigh just as much.

Not to be deterred by humiliation, I spent much of my house time trying to get my numbers down. Among others, I tried a Wii game where you run up and down in place, propelling a cartoon bicycle around a cartoon bike route. Much like my real pedaling prowess, I ran into walls and fell off a lot, but the virtual version hurts less.

I also tried games where I hit soccer balls with my head and did aerobics with a class full of cartoon competitors, none of whom were panting and gasping for air like I was. Wii are not fit, indeed.

However, I'm happy to report that by last week, my numbers were actually coming down, along with my cartoon age. I'm now just a baby whale. Actually, I've come to respect the Wii Fit and for the first time in my entire life I am exercising. Amazing what a little animated peer pressure can do.

Also, barometric pressure. As the weather got worse, temperatures teetering between 20 and 37 degrees, we all got to stay home and watch the Olympics. It's a shame we couldn't sell snow to Vancouver where they needed it. Meanwhile, what's the deal with curling? It's like a combination of shuffled board and housework, where you fling the granite stone and use the mop and glo to sweep it down court. I could never work up much excitement about the game but it did make me snicker.

I loved watching the ski jump events. The majesty of a young athlete soaring through the air was exhilarating. As luck would have it, there's a ski jump balance exercise on my Wii Fit too. I'd crouch on the platform in front of the TV, watch the cartoon skier coming down the chute and then quickly straighten my knees (crackle) when I thought I should jump. Wheeeeee!

Most times the cartoon Fay could be seen rolling ass over tea kettle in the snow, but every once in a while I jumped just right and flew like a champ. When I finished, the Wii totaled my score and announced I was "unbalanced." I've heard that before.

When it was passable outside but still not a great idea to go driving hither and yon, we spent several evenings hosting friends or going to friends' homes. In the old days it was Studio 54 or any number of dance clubs; now it's Wii bowling in somebody's living room. Simultaneously, the Tea Baggers and Conservative PAC people were out on the West Coast boozing it up and consorting with call girls while the gay people were all sitting around playing Wii – what's wrong with this picture????

I do have to ask if there's a correlation between Wii bowling and the crush of people having rotator cuff surgery. Just sayin'.

One night it was hilarious. After dining on a 2300 calorie dinner, we tried the Wii's virtual hula hoops to work off 11 calories each. Amid shouts of "Align your pelvis, baby!" and "Work it! Work it! Work it!" the soundtrack recalled days on the disco dance floor. Back then we'd hit the diner for a nightcap. Now we're lucky it's not drinking contrast dye before an MRI at the hospital.

Along with the closing ceremonies for the Olympics, I know we are all anxious to see the closing ceremonies from this disgustingly cold and blizzard-filled winter. Even our pals who escaped to Florida were rewarded with cold feet. It was warmer in Canada. Let's face it, Spring Fever could be a pandemic this year.

Okay, winter, go on now, go walk out the door, just turn around now, 'cause you're not welcome anymore, I will survive. Hey, Hey.

As a matter of fact, let's chill the brew to fight bone loss and get out the summer clothes. They are going to look great, because after all, Wii Fit!▼

April 2010

Home Improvement shows are like pornography. Watching them makes you do things you shouldn't do. Like tiling the bathroom floor.

"How difficult is this project?" I asked my handy spouse as we watched DIY porn on Saturday morning.

"It's easy."

After 28 years you'd think I'd know better. I'm surprised nobody showed up to try and sell me the Brooklyn Bridge. Frankly, it would have cost less.

Since we already had the floor tiles, all we needed was concrete board to go under the tile. And grout, a trowel, a grout sponge, adhesive, concrete board screws, and an appointment to have my head examined.

They call it concrete board because it emits concrete dust that sticks to your clothing like powdered sugar. It's also called concrete board because two old dykes cannot lift a sheet of it into the car by themselves without developing sciatica.

Meanwhile back at the ranch house, Bonnie wanted to avoid crawling under the house to shut off the water. So she convinced me we'd just cut out the back of the under-sink cabinet to remove it without fooling with the water supply. Well, sawing a hole in the cabinet made a filthy mess but we got it out of the bathroom without incident. Sadly, it turned out that the turnoff valve on the toilet was broken, so removing the porcelain horse would have caused a geyser. See Bonnie run. See Bonnie slither under the house to turn the water off.

I married for better or worse, but not for carting a toilet through the house. It poured more liquid on my floor than visiting dogs. If I wanted to wash my hands I had to use ice cubes. See the consequences of watching porn?

Next came removal of the backsplash from the sink, half of which was the leaning tower of formica, having become unglued over a decade ago. I became unglued when the remaining section, which must have been fastened with Gorilla Glue, was removed, taking a chunk of wall board with it. Great, now we have to repaint the room. It's amazing how the destruction phase of these projects goes awry so fast.

Back to Lowes for the part to fix the toilet cut-off so we can turn the water on again. By 3 p.m. we had the water fixed and one sheet of concrete board on the bathroom floor. By 4 p.m. we had screwed it in place. By 5 p.m. we had cocktails and called it a day.

DAY TWO OF THE ONE-DAY PROJECT

Broke several drill bits on the concrete board. Back to Lowes. Second board screwed into place. Fay and Bonnie screwed because we are out of time. Must put project on hold for two days. The sink and toilet are in the hall, we have to clean up our master bathroom in case guests have to pee. The house is a construction site.

DAY FIVE OF THE ONE-DAY PROJECT

Little details like Bonnie's employment supersede construction. Back to work on the floor now. After painstakingly trimming one tile to fit around where the toilet would be if it wasn't in the hall, we determine that everything is easy with the right tools – and we don't have them. We rent a tile cutter and race home, playing beat the clock to cut all the tiles before nightfall when the rented machine turns into a pumpkin or costs us another $44. We make it. Huzzah!

DAY SIX OF THE ONE-DAY PROJECT

Great. A narrow slice of concrete board is sticking out past the tile, infringing on the space for the door sill. Gotta trim that concrete board. Did I mention concrete dust?

Bonnie took a jigsaw to the offending concrete board and blew a cloud of thick white fog up to the ceiling and back down into every crevice and onto every surface in the whole house.

We've got concrete dust in the dog food bowls, on the bedspreads, in the computer keyboards. We could scribble %&*% DIY in concrete dust on the tabletops. Auuggghhh!!!! Now we need a cleaning service.

Off to buy a sill to fit between bathroom and hall. Got a cheap metal one and it looked like crap next to the tiles. Back to Lowes yet again, where we lost our marbles and bought a black marble sill. That sucking sound was the ATM.

DAY SEVEN OF THE ONE-DAY PROJECT

Bonnie mixed the adhesive and began meticulously setting tiles in place. With each subsequent tile the glue got thicker and thicker, setting up faster than she could possibly set tiles. Pretty soon she's tiling like the sorcerer's apprentice and cursing like a sailor trying to finish before her putty knife turns to the sword in the stone. She didn't make it. Out of usable glue, out of time. Toss bucket and embedded putty knife in trash.

TIME OUT

Here, the story detours. Project on hold for a quick trip out of town. Arrived back on Sunday night and by Monday morning both of us are struck down with world-class food poisoning. Beebe Hospital visit required. I will spare you the details but remind you that one of our two toilets was sitting useless in the hall. Timing is everything. In so many ways.

DAY SEVENTEEN OF THE ONE DAY PROJECT

We're grouting now, with a brand new putty knife. Decided it was silly to put back the old cabinet with the holes in the back for the water pipes so we bought a new, decorative cabinet with new hardware. While we're at it (it's the *while-your-at-its* that will kill you) we're looking at a new granite countertop and decorative sink because we have to hide the wall gouges where the old formica ripped off.

Ripped off, did we say? The new cabinet is in place but the drawers won't open because we got a lefty not a righty and upon opening the drawers they hit the door jam. Can't move the cabinet the offending *one measly inch* because water pipes won't move. Call the plumber to move the pipes, begging him to hurry because company is coming in three days. Exercise the credit card.

DAY NINETEEN OF THE MANHATTAN PROJECT

Buy paint and new baseboards. Close the bathroom door to keep the dogs from exploring unfinished baseboard areas. Wait! The door won't close. Tiles are too high. To sand the door down we have to take it off its hinges.

Fay becomes unhinged. See Bonnie and Fay schlepping the toilet and sink back into the bathroom. See an expensive cleaning crew come get concrete dust off every tchotchke in the house.

Fay and Bonnie are now in rehab for their addiction to Do-It-Yourself projects. HGTV is porn. Pure and simple. I'm swearing off. Or am I just swearing?▼

THANKS FOR THE MAMMARIES

PRE-QUAKE SUNDAY

Boobquake. Did you hear about it? At first I thought it referred to the massive tsunami of GOP blather against Obama's latest legislation. But no, it meant actual boobs, as in mammaries. And it happened on Monday, April 26.

On the preceding day I was enjoying brunch with a gaggle of friends when somebody mentioned the upcoming Boobquake. Apparently I'd been under a rock and had so far missed the whole boob-ha-ha.

I grabbed my Blackberry and surfed. Sure enough, a Boobquake Facebook page told of a worldwide protest against an Iranian cleric's suggestion that immodestly dressed women cause earthquakes. He blames the women for causing lascivious thoughts from men, resulting in fornication and adultery, which, in turn, cause earthquakes.

Puleeeze. Joining the brain trust of Pat Robertson (lesbians caused Hurricane Katrina) and Fred Phelps (God hates Fags) we have Hojatoleslam Kazem Sedighi causing a Boobquake. Wow, his first name is a mouthful, and everyone knows that more than a mouthful is wasted, but I digress.

Sedighi, Teheran's Friday prayer leader, pissed off Purdue college student Jen McCreight, who put a Facebook page together urging women worldwide to satirize the cleric on the following Monday by revealing a little cleavage – or ankle, for the modest.

"Sedighi claims that not dressing modestly causes earthquakes," said McCreight, "If so, we should be able to test this claim scientifically. Time for a Boobquake." So she told her Facebook friends that on Monday, April 26th, she would wear her most cleavage-showing shirt and they should too, in order to have some fun with the hateful cleric.

Hmmmm. A scientific call to arms, or breasts as the case may be. Okay, I was locked and loaded. Frankly, I'm afraid we were all a little loaded at brunch, having Mimosa'd our way through this perky conversation, some of us amply prepared for a seismic wave of breast activism and others fretting about lack of ammunition to get the job done. "Who gives a hooter?" we all agreed. We're in!

Richter Scales and bra sizes aside, the planned boobquake caught my imagination. And I was not alone. Twenty-four hours after it was first announced, 40,000 Facebook people (or 80,000 juggies, give or take) in dozens of countries had signed on for this most civil disobedience; a major magnitude of tectonic titties.

It made the papers, too. I loved the headlines "Vancouver protesters plan to shake beliefs with Boobquake," "Cleric vs. Cleavage," or NBC's "Boobquake lifts and separates political opinion." The punny headlines went wild. By Sunday at 3 p.m. *New York* magazine reported that 120,000 women signed on to show cleavage, dress less modestly, and otherwise give the raspberries to the Imam.

Oh, the aftershocks! I tweeted and Facebooked my participation, and heard "Keep us abreast," Do man boobs count?" (um...not sure) and my favorite "you work at home, so just the schnauzers will see your cleavage!"

No, I intended to hang out, if you'll excuse the expression at Walmart and the liquor store, too, busting out all over town. A gal's gotta do what a gal's gotta do to combat these idiotic religious wing nuts trying to blame natural disasters on their idea of unnatural behavior. Did they blame the Icelandic volcano on their plumbers bending over under the sink??? I didn't think so. No, this is just your every day fundamentalist cleric misogyny.

MONDAY, A REAL BOOBQUAKE

Got up early to discover hundreds of thousands of women worldwide set to expose their breasts in varying degrees. Jen McCreight was online reminding everyone that this is not about baring all, but baring whatever you feel comfy baring.

She will be in a tank top. I donned my CAMP Rehoboth sweat shirt and made sure the zipper was down dangerously low over my bare skin.

Will this seismic boobie wave make the earth move under my feet? Wait a minute. In my world, attractive sights like this can make the earth move. Well, I guess if the earth moves for you in a good way, that's fine. Death and destruction as described by the Imam, not so much.

Oh no! By 8 a.m. FOX Noise reported an earthquake in Taiwan! Could the politically incorrect Imam be seismically correct? Luckily, Boobquake founder McCreight had previously posted "I know many earthquakes happen on a daily basis, so we're looking to see if Boobquake significantly increases the number or magnitude of earthquakes." NBC reported that once the Boobquake is over, McCreight will be researching earthquake statistics to see if there actually was an uptick in seismic activity.

Well, here it is 4 p.m. on Monday and our planet has not yet been destroyed by this wanton display of womanity. And so far there has been little fallout seismic-wise. I've had no word on any other kind of fall-out, but needless to say, with a globe full of gals in low cut garments, flaunting their assets, somebody somewhere must have had a wardrobe malfunction. Hey, if a breast falls out in the forest and the Imam isn't there to see it, is he still stupid?

All I know is that on my drive-by at the bank, my promenade through Walmart's check-out line or my wicked sashay around the car to pump some gas, no fault lines erupted and Rehoboth didn't quake into the ocean. Thanks to the cold and damp weather, the only scientific data I can quantify is one pair of boobs making its, er, point to the silly, delusional Imam.

Enough. How long are we going to have to put up with hate-filled boobs like these?▼

A ROLLING HOME GATHERS NO MOSS...

Okay, I lied. In a winter *Letters* post I vowed never again to travel from Florida to Reho on Route I-95 any other way than by wide-bodied jet—my days of making the hideous drive were over.

Woman plans and God laughs hysterically. Bonnie and I drove that same ugly highway again in March, on the maiden voyage of our craziest idea yet.

Following our customary pattern of upending our entire lives every decade or so, we've done it again. In the '80s we bought a boat (a hole in the water into which you throw money); in the '90s we moved the vessel to Rehoboth Bay (Ruddertown steel drums at 1 a.m. UGH!) ; at the dawn of the Millennium we moved ourselves full-time to Rehoboth (okay, so who needs a decent paying job anyway?); and now we're on the move and downwardly mobile once again.

Of course, we would never leave Gayberry RFD permanently – it will always be base CAMP – but open road here we come. Rather than being the sisterhood of the traveling pants we are now the sisterhood of the traveling house – a 27-foot land yacht. Ever financially imprudent, we've bought a great big depreciating asset.

RV? Camping? Really? If this seems oxymoronic for this writer, if not plain moronic, let me explain the difference between camping and RVing. It's the same as the difference between camping and boating. While a certain amount of gear schlepping and bug spray is still involved, the chief difference is that boat or RV, there is carpet between your bed and your toilet. Civility.

We knew we'd take to RV life instantly. Good thing, too, because due to circumstances beyond our control we had only 45 minutes of flight instruction before leaving Tampa for the journey home in the Hindenburg. Gentlewomen, rev your engines.

Naturally I was assigned shotgun, while Thelma took the wheel, guiding our wide load (and its wide loads) down the highway.

"Do you feel like bus driver Ralph Kramden?" I asked.

"A little," she said.

"Well, luckily you don't look like him, although your plan to stop at Waffle House later might change that."

"One of these days, Alice, right in the kisser."

I gotta hand it to Bonnie. She was fearless. We considered ourselves lucky we didn't take out mailboxes and parked cars on both sides of the street as our blimp lumbered towards I-95. But within minutes my spouse had expertly judged the Titanic's midsection, checked out the giant funhouse mirrors flanking the bus and learned to love the back-up camera.

We set out at 8:30 a.m. and by noon, when we pulled into the Waffle House parking lot, Bonnie was driving the thing like it was a Mini-Cooper.

By nightfall we stayed in our first KOA Kampground, although we did learn that RVs can stay overnight for free in Walmart parking lots (really!). We also conquered our virgin fumblings with plug-in electric, leveling the rig and battery management – all without threat of divorce.

The good news is that unlike the boat, our new lodging has a queen size walk-around bed in the back – a far cry from the boat's aft cabin bunks where, to get into bed, we had to crawl on our bellies. Today, more than a decade later, that would not be pretty, if even possible.

"Is it like the RV in *Meet the Fockers*? " asked a friend. No, our new house on wheels is not an ostentatious, over-the-top ridiculous rig like Barbra Streisand and Dustin Hoffman drove, but it suits these fockers well. And it does have a satellite TV antenna. Priorities.

Come morning we took off again and learned a lesson. Like a boat, it is prudent to secure all contents when underway. Braking for a red light sent a 2-lb bag of M&M Peanuts rolling everywhere like little chocolate marbles (former owners, forgive us; we cleaned up every speck!). From now on we batten the hatches.

Well, we made it back to Rehoboth swiftly and without incident, M&M avalanche notwithstanding. Our return did require a quick stop at Cape Henlopen campground for a sewer hook-up. No, we did not suffer Chevy Chase's disgusting fate in his vacation movie, although Bonnie exacted her revenge for my Ralph Kramden comment. She enlisted me to stand with my foot holding down the hose while we emptied our tank. Once I was firmly in place she ran, laughing, 50 yards away from the stench. Next time I'll get you, my little pretty.

Soon after, we took a second shake-down trip, this time to Chincoteague, VA. We did not swim with the horses, but hung with the Schnauzers, overlooking the water and lighthouse, enjoying the tranquility of our first weekend at a campsite.

Actually we spent most of our time traipsing back and forth between the campsite and ACE Hardware, a mile down the road, hunting things we didn't know we needed until we needed them. By Sunday night we were exhausted but well-equipped.

Now, as we plan our first big trip – a three week Canadian adventure mid-July, we both lust after any excuse to use the rig again before then. Short of overnighting at the Old Landing Road Walmart, we are considering a night down at Indian River, supervising the new bridge construction.

Bonnie did go for a drive in the RV recently when she brought the dogs to our Maryland vet for teeth cleaning. She delivered the dental patients in her own personal waiting room complete with her personal selection of magazines and snacks. Of course, between the fuel bill and the dental bill, we're in the poor house, but at least it's got a queen size bed and plush carpet.

Now that we've entered the world of RV accessories like load levelers, ez hitches and a variety of clamps, coils and hoses (a hole in the highway into which you pour money?) we should have our heads examined. Wave if you see us on the road. I haven't decided which name to stencil on the back: Fay's Folly or Bonnie's Boondoggle. It remains to be seen. Hum it with me, "Trailer for sale or rent, queens of the road...." ▼

In the amazing world of gay, lesbian, bisexual and transgender publishing, with many of our niche books going mainstream and having a straight as well as gay following, our corner of the publishing world seems to be thriving where others are not. And the Lambda Literary Society, a non-profit set up to nurture and promote gay writing and its writers is leading the way.

So it was a grand night in New York City at the Lambda Literary Awards May 28, as a super-supportive audience of writers, publishers, editors, agents, readers and many other friends of LGBT writing cheered, applauded and occasionally felt moved to standing ovations.

Lesbian comic, social commentator and author Kate Clinton was awarded the Lambda Literary Pioneer Award for her long-time body of hilarious, but more importantly, activist work – her speech was hilarious as well, calling herself and her gal pal the last unmarried, childless, petless lesbians in the world.

My favorite moments included JM Redmann winning the lesbian mystery category with her new novel *Death of a Dying Man*, bringing back the wonderful PI Mickey Knight for another adventure. In her speech, she noted the marvelous glut of books for and by LGBT writers – "There are so many books they can't possibly burn them all." The audience cheered.

The lesbian romance category was won by Colette Moody and her wildly imaginative novel *The Sublime and Spirited Voyage of the Original Sin*. Fast-paced, funny, sexy and simply deliciously written, it's a must-read. But no more so than all five finalists in the category – *Worth Every Step* by KG MacGregor, a romantic adventure that combines climbing Mt. Kilimanjaro and one of the most honestly written coming out struggles ever; *It Should Be a Crime* by Carsen Taite – campus and courtroom romance and a bit of mystery, wrapped in a hot love story;

Stepping Stones by Karin Kallmaker, giving readers a birds eye view from the Hollywood sign to a sexy romp of a studio romance. Rounding out the category is *No Rules of Engagement* by Tracey Richardson – a very topical and expertly written romance with a military setting and terrifically drawn characters. Read 'em all!

Full disclosure here: I was asked to be a judge for the Romance category, and what a pleasure it was. I hunkered down for the unusually snowy Rehoboth winter and read dozens of books. Some were just okay, lots were entertaining and fun, and the cream easily rose to the top. It was a grand experience. I have to give an extra nod to two books that I also loved in that category: *Fireside* by Cate Culpepper (wonderful story and excellently drawn characters) and *Erosistible* by Gill McNight – just plain fun!

It was great to hear from Lambda Board President Katherine Forrest, *Boys in the Band* author Mart Crowley winning his first award ever ('bout time!) and comments from so many others in the industry. Not only was it a grand night in the Big Apple, but the Lammys proved once again, that LGBT writers and publishers (Go Bella and Bold Strokes and Bywater and more!) are prolific, determined and hardworking in the face of a changing publishing industry.

Get your summer read on!▼

MY NAME IS FAY J AND I AM A CARBOHOLIC

After a fabulous weekend in New Orleans back in May I went into detox to dry out. And I'm not talking about alcohol, although I probably had more to drink those four days than was prudent. No, I'm talking about carbohydrates. For me, it's not the demon rum, it's the demon bun.

While my pals headed to the airport wondering if the three ounces of last-minute liquid they consumed in the cab would be allowed through security in their carry-on stomachs, I was climbing back on the wagon from a binge of another sort altogether. I'd had an endless excess of beignets, fried seafood, indulgent desserts and yes, the astonishing sugar content of the bottomless Hurricane cocktails I slurped. I was using again.

But bad as my Crescent City bender was, I'm lucky. Thanks to a fairly recent revelation, I can admit to my addiction. My name is Fay Jacobs and I'm a carboholic. And while I have been called a humorist a time or two, this is not really meant to be funny. Sure, I see humor in the situation, but really, this is pretty serious stuff.

Years ago, I wrote in this column about my battle of the bulge. "I've tried every diet ever invented and they all work. Scarsdale, Weight Watchers, the cantaloupe diet, you name it. I can lose lots of weight on all of them. Unfortunately, I don't, because I invariably fall off the wagon and onto the buffet table.

The only real success I ever had was during the Phen-Fen diet pill craze. In three months I shed thirty five pounds, and a lifetime of guilt. It was terrific. But next thing I knew, doctors started shrieking that our heart valves were becoming apple-sauce and wham, the government confiscated my Phen-Fen. Luckily, the only permanent medical damage I suffered was blowing back up into a women's world shopper."

Honestly, I thought I was hopeless. Years ago, one sadistic doctor reported his diagnosis. "You have an overactive fork." Hilarious bastard. But you know, it may have been true. And I worried about my health. Not to mention my health insurance rates. My body mass index was higher than my credit score.

Then, last summer, somebody suggested I might actually be addicted to carbs. I don't mean overly fond of, I mean addicted. Physically, medically, Betty Ford-addicted. I had a habit. Compulsive is not too strong a term.

As I pondered the possibility of real dependence, I attempted to cut most carbs – bread, potatoes and fried foods, from my current diet, if you could call that kind of gluttony a diet. And I went cold turkey. Literally, because cold turkey was one of the few things I could still eat. And it was difficult, bordering on painful, confining myself to salads, meats, fish and veggies, surrounded, as we are, by buckets of beach fries and funnel cakes.

The first few days were a bitch and so was I. Grumpy R Us. It was really, really hard. I struggled. But as the days and weeks went by, honestly, it got easier. The further I got from pizza and pasta, the more appealing healthy eating became. If somebody told me a year ago I would ever happily pass up a club sandwich for a Caesar salad I would have called them delusional.

But here's the real revelation. Over the past year, when I did relapse or treat myself to something verboten, I *immediately* wanted more of it, like some ravenous animal. Had a slice, craved a sandwich; ate the sandwich, wanted spaghetti. Really, really wanted it. I felt myself losing control, craving a dopamine high from French Toast or French Dips. This addiction hypothesis was quickly becoming established fact.

So fast forward. After a little less than twelve months avoiding excess carbs I have lost 32 pounds. My spouse and friends have provided peer support and been champs for noticing my success and encouraging me. "I can see the weight loss in your face," they all said. That's because all 32 pounds came off my jowls. It will take another two years to come off my thighs. But it's progress.

And I seem to be keeping the weight off. I'm writing this, not to congratulate myself, but to share what I consider to be this bizarre secret about carb addiction. Maybe some of our readers are addicted, too. And of course, in my feeble attempts at addiction metaphors, I mean no disrespect to my readers battling more traditionally discussed addictions of their own.

I'm also very lucky that this particular addiction only makes me burp and reach for the menu, rather than buying illegal substances or behaving badly towards people I love. But believe me, there are scary parallels.

So I'm in detox and on the wagon. I'm committed to getting the carbs out of my system again. And I'm sharing this with you at risk of having everybody watch what I eat from now on. Jeepers, I'm the restaurant writer for this magazine, for pity's sake. Well, I'll just have to taste only a bite or two from now on and hope I can stay clean.

May the proof be in the sugar-free pudding. ▼

June 2010

I got something in my craw this morning, and like a feline hair ball, I have to cough it up. In this case I am using my column as a literary Heimlich Maneuver.

What's with people? It's 2010 and a vicious double standard exists – so much that even our allies fall prey to it when discussing LGBT equality. And I'm not even talking about big subjects like gay marriage or gays in the military.

No, I'm talking about an everyday reaction to something like boobs on the beach. From what I understand, a couple of transitioning transgender females – in this case that would be men who are transitioning to women, but who have only gotten top surgery so far. Still with me?

Well apparently, these transitioning women decided to show off their new tits at Poodle Beach last weekend. And, as they should have done, the Rehoboth summer police requested that the exhibitionists put their bathing suit tops back on. That's because under Rehoboth ordinances, it is illegal to show female breasts on the beach, no matter who is wearing them on their chests.

Fair enough, I say, although the attitudes in Europe regarding this issue are more progressive and more to my liking. Frankly, since the ordinance relates to female boobs only, I hope those trans women know they will be getting their male privilege lopped off along with their privates.

But female boobs are to stay covered on our beaches. It's the law. And that should go for trans women with female breasts as well as any other woman with female breasts. After a bit of a boob-haha on the beach, the show-offs did put their clothes back on and that was that.

But it wasn't. In a phone call to CAMP Rehoboth, someone made the comment "Well, this doesn't help our cause," referring to the continuing quest for LGBT equality in Delaware.

Excuuuuuse me??????? Okay, I know what the caller meant. Homophobes will have a field day with the story and it's already been the talk of Rehoboth talk radio and a great howler for bigots everywhere throughout the county.

But it really pisses me off (can you tell?) that the cause of heterosexuals everywhere was not damaged by a coinciding news report of a group of drunken straight people vomiting off hotel balconies and trashing lodging establishments. No, no, their cause, the reputation of straight people, was not denigrated a bit. While just the boob story made talk radio, I heard nothing about the straight people urinating in the street, the drunken idiot who led police on a dangerous high speed chase through almost all of Ocean City or the goofball who got tired of walking and stole a bike. You are not going to hear TV's talking heads shouting "Damn heterosexuals!"

And as if this didn't gag me enough, a second caller complained that two women were spotted in the surf at Olive Avenue behaving like randy teenagers in the backseat of a car. Frankly, I'm as nauseous as the next person over especially enthusiastic public displays of affection but I don't want to see frantic groping and a human rutting season played out in front of me, gay or straight. Don't want to see it.

But don't you dare tell me that while you are not prejudiced, one is worse than the other.

I am sick and tired of having gay people who misbehave used as a cudgel against our civil rights efforts. I am sick of having our morons (and we have them) used against us while their morons (and they have them) get a pass. Joey Buttafuoco did not set back anybody's civil rights but his own. Don't gay people have the right to have our own nincompoops without putting our *human rights* in jeopardy? I think it just goes to our forefathers' expectation of Americans having the right to life, liberty and the pursuit of happiness. There should be a codicil – the right to make a complete ass of yourself, whatever your orientation, gender, religion or ethnicity without taking your whole minority group with you. Either that or we have to make sure that majority groups take it on the chin for their lowest common denominators too.

It reminds me of the story I heard from the Cape Henlopen State Police one time. Two gals were at North Shores with their bathing suit tops off. A park officer asked them to put the tops back on as there was an ordinance against being topless.

The girls obeyed, but quickly disrobed again when the officer was out of sight. He returned to warn them a second time and they obeyed but gave the officer a lot of lip, threatening to claim anti-gay discrimination. The third time the officer showed up, he ordered the women to put their clothes on and escorted the pair off the beach – to the cheers of the rest of the lesbians on the sand.

Rules are rules, gay or straight, and please don't blame me for the flawed judgment of my brothers and sisters. My fitness for equality should not be an issue at all, but since it is, do not judge me by the actions of a couple of clownish kids who just happen to be transgender. That's as wrong as my entire womanhood being judged because there's a murderous woman on death row, or my Jewishness denigrated because of that cruel bastard Bernie Madoff.

Discuss.

There. I can swallow better now. ▼

WHAT'S UP WITH YOUR VUVUZELA?

Do you have one? Can you toot it?

If you don't know what I'm talking about, you may have been under a rock for the past month.

The vuvuzela is a South African plastic horn, made in China, used for cheering on soccer teams, or as they call the sport in that country, football. The appearance of the foot-long, brightly colored plastic trumpet in the stands at the World Cup has created quite a buzz. Literally. When blown by thousands of fans simultaneously, the resulting, insistent hum sounds like swarms of very angry bees. A single vuvuzela blast sounds like an elephant looking for a date.

Thousands of vuvuzela-equipped soccer fans have driven much of the on-site fans, television feeds and play-by-play announcers bonkers. The constant blowing of the vuvuzela in the stands during the games has become both an international joke and an international incident. Swarms of angry people are turning off television coverage of the games because they cannot stand the droning vuvuzela onslaught. How the players on the field concentrate, I have no idea.

Then, the media went on a toot. For days now I've been unable to watch the news without seeing one or more usually dignified anchors attempting to make rude Vuvu sounds at the camera. If that wasn't amusing enough, the marketing folks have gotten into the act. There is already a Vuvuzela App for the iPhone, so you can toot your $300 vuvuzela along with the $3 plastic ones. Wait, there are several apps available, multiplying like rabbits.

According to Wikipedia, the vuvuzela, used to be called the lepatata, also a great word ("I'll show you my lepatata if you show me your vuvuzela.") and the instrument has been the object of concern for a while. It's been said that the high sound pressure levels at close range can lead to permanent hearing loss for unprotected ears. I'm sure soccer fans are not happy buying an expensive ticket to sit in the stands, followed by purchasing expensive Bose noise-canceling headphones.

With vuvuzela news all over the media, somebody thought it was a good idea to give out free vuvuzelas at a recent Florida Marlins baseball game. Predictably, Marlin second baseman Dan Uggla said, "that was the worst handout or giveaway I've ever been a part of in baseball." Frankly, the Marlins record is nothing to toot about.

Naturally, Facebook has a vuvulela page and now there is Vuvuzela Radio, a station dedicated to playing the sound of the vuvuzela," non-stop, without commercial breaks, so you can get your full daily dose: anywhere, anytime." I think it's a joke but I am not sure. You can, if you must, buy a vuvuzela online at dozens of sites, along with mousepads that say "vuvuzela-free zone" and other vuvu stuff.

So the world is still abuzz with the vuvuzela, fans galore are fighting the urge to mute the games, engineers everywhere are figuring out ways to filter out the annoying buzz from broadcasts and comics everywhere are having a field day. The Vuvu's 15 minutes of fame ticks away. Hey, by the time you read this, you may not even remember the vuvu-ha over the whole thing.

A friend of mine insists that Vuvuzela was a drag queen back in the 80s. Who's to argue?▼

July 2010

Everybody has secrets and some are bigger than others.

I had one back in high school. It was the mid-'60s, and I was the good little girl, dating boys, wearing heels and repressing a sexual orientation I didn't even have a name for. Did I know? I think so. Did I admit it, even to myself? No way.

I joined the high school drama club (or, as comic Jaffee Cohen once called it, "gay head start") and had a ton of friends. Among them was a girl named Carmen.

Even then, 1965, she was an out lesbian, although no one used the word. She held hands with girls and both fascinated and terrified me. Some of my friends warned me to stay away from Carmen – she was, "you know, 'funny.' One of them." The '60s counter-culture may have been about to explode, but gays were still closeted, feared and shunned.

But I didn't stay away from Carmen. We were in school plays together, at cast parties, running around Greenwich Village, me playing the guitar at amateur nights in the clubs, Carmen and our other friends singing along. We were casual friends, friendly acquaintances. There were rehearsals and school lunch hours and staying over at our friends' houses. Underage drinking, too. Did Carmen and I ever mix it up? No. But I think there was one night when it was awfully, awfully, and tantalizingly close.

And then we graduated, everyone went separate ways and I continued on my repressive road for many mostly miserable years. And my frightening senior-year fascination with a butch dyke named Carmen was something I never ever breathed a word about to a single soul. Until right this minute as I type these words.

After high school I went to college in D.C., dated guys, did the "right" thing, got married, changed my name, got divorced, kept my married name because of my directing career, and finally came out of the closet a long, unhappy 14 years after high school.

Fast forward to a June 2010 lesbian/bisexual writer's conference in Orlando. Of course, at this point I could not be *more* out – a lesbian author and advocate plus being happily same-sex married for almost 30 years. Life takes its own path in its own sweet time. And now is a sweet time for me.

At this conference, I taught a class on humor-writing and did some readings from my books. Flipping through the conference program I saw the sad news of the passing of a long-time bookstore owner and writer, named Ruth.

Following my class, as I talked with author, publisher and reader friends, I spied folks going over to give their condolences to the lone man at the conference – Chris, Ruth's husband, who was there in her stead. I, too, went over to extend my sympathies, telling him I remembered his wife from a visit I made to their bookstore in Albuquerque.

A few minutes later, as I was chatting with friends, I saw Chris moving towards me with a spectacularly funny look on his face. "Hey," he called. "Did you go to high school in New York?"

"Yes, I did."

"Rhodes Prep School?"

"Exactly." He had my attention.

"Fay. From Drama Club. You played Maggie in *The Man Who Came to Dinner*?"

"Yes," I said cautiously, amazed that a 41-year old connection was being offered and wondering why Chris knew me and I couldn't place him. It was a small school and an even smaller drama department.

"Omigod," said Chris, "I was listening to you talk and I knew I recognized your voice. I'm Carmen, I mean I was, Carmen."

Oh. My. God. Carmen. I stared. I grinned. I stared some more at the handsome, mustached man before me. He stared and grinned back. I thought my head might explode. Carmen.

We headed for the nearest bar in the hotel to share much needed full-strength cocktails and catch up.

I know that my path to coming out was long and filled with angst. But Carmen, now Chris, made, what seems to me, a much harder, riskier, but in the end, quicker path toward authenticity. Right after graduation Carmen made a decision considered brave today, so I cannot imagine the courage it took in the late sixties.

She, soon he, left home immediately, moved to an East Village hotel, and began finding ways of obtaining black market male hormones. He worked at the infamous 82 Club where performers were all drag queens; waiters tuxedo-wearing dykes. Soon, he was fortunate to find a medical study to accept him and provide the testosterone legally and under medical supervision. Carmen became Chris and never looked back.

Well actually, he did look back long enough to return to our high school and have his legally-changed name put into his transcripts so he could go to college. He moved out West, met Ruth and they lived happily as husband and wife for 30 years, until her sad passing in April.

Over inhibition-banishing alcohol, we easily recalled high school friends and events – the casting of our production of *Dracula*, the night we listened from the sidewalk on West 4th Street to the sounds of the Lovin' Spoonful before they were famous; the students who drove us crazy in drama club; our wonderful friend Mary, my friend to this day, whose stunning beauty was attractive to us both. And the sad loss of at least two of our drama club colleagues to 80s-era AIDS.

You know, as a writer, I always use the LGBT alphabet to describe my community. And while I advocate for and admire the transsexuals in our population I have had precious little personal contact with trans men and women. Finding Chris has had a profound impact on me.

Here is a man mourning the loss of his spouse of thirty years, so happy is an inappropriate word to describe him. I have empathy for his loss as he grieves and tries, I would hope, eventually to move on—made all the more difficult by his being a trans man. I know that often neither the straight nor the lesbian community is welcoming, and as he said to me, "I'm 61 and transgender. I don't expect anything to be easy."

Probably not. But for me, I want to use the word happy to describe the choice Chris made over forty years ago. He was desperately unhappy being made to live as woman, just a girl, really, and was willing to buck all of society, and sadly, his own family, to become the man he knew himself to be.

For what my opinion is worth, I am so proud of him. And for this Pride season and beyond, I have a new and personal connection to the T in LGBT. I hope Chris and I can stay in touch. I'd like that. But frankly, I hope he doesn't tell any of our mutual friends what a god awful actress I was back in our pre-*Glee* high school days. That's one secret we should keep.

Life can be much stranger than fiction. And more surprising and wonderful, too. ▼

BETTER HIM THAN ME, BUT STILL...

Diabetes is epidemic and not just in humans. A few months ago, my 11-year old Schnauzer Paddy was diagnosed as seriously diabetic. Naturally my spouse and I were upset, but ultimately reassured that with proper diet and medication Paddy could continue to live a normal, active doghood. As for me, I considered this just one more case of that which does not kill us makes us giggle.

We're standing at the pharmacy counter, having handed the vet's prescription to the clerk, when she absently asked the routine questions.

"Birthdate?"

"Um, March 17, 1999."

"Phone number?"

"He doesn't have a phone."

"Well, are you his guardian?"

"I guess so."

"So I can reach the patient on your phone?"

"Well you can, but he won't have much to say." What part of the words Animal Hospital on the prescription was she having trouble understanding?

"Oh," she said, distractedly, "what kind of syringes will he be using?"

"I don't think he will be using any kind. He doesn't have opposable thumbs."

Please let the clerk be paying more attention to the Insulin dose than the species of the patient it was written for.

"He's a Schnauzer. Hello???" We all laughed.

Back home, my kitchen counter looks like the ICU, with medicine vials, syringes and a great big container labeled "Hazardous Medical Waste" for discarded needles. I haven't seen this much drug paraphernalia since Cheech & Chong. And of course we have new low fat, low carb food, available only by prescription from the veterinarian as well. I should probably try it myself.

Naturally, one of the two of us in the house with opposable thumbs needed to learn how to administer the injections. Want to guess who that would be? I got queasy watching *Dr. Quinn Medicine Woman* so I deferred to Nurse Ratched.

My spouse was a natural at it, and the patient perked right up after just a few days of treatment. Paddy's brother Moxie has no idea that when his delicious fatty dog food is used up, he too will be dining fat free – and I feel no compunction to tell him that his Burger King flavored kibble will soon become rice cakes.

I have to say, it's probably easier for Paddy to keep his sugar under control than it is for his human counterparts. I mean he's not given to sneaking a Snickers bar or having too many martinis like some members of his family.

But Paddy's diagnosis did present a new problem. The dogs had never been kenneled, always enjoying slumber parties with their friends when we went away. Now, all of a sudden, twice daily injections are involved and we have entered the world of pet hotels affiliated with veterinary facilities.

Hold onto your ATM card, Batman, no saving money here with the Travelocity gnome. These places rival the Ritz-Carlton Dubai. And funny, even when I go to a Motel 6 I don't have to show proof of a distemper shot, though I've had plenty of distemper there.

Frankly, my guys have now been treated to five star accommodations. They got a choice of a Standard or Deluxe room, or the Deluxe Suite, which has more square footage than my guest room. And it's not even double occupancy. Moxie pays full price and his brother pays half. In total, it's more per night than a Red Roof Inn.

Of course, I made sure to request non-smoking. And when they told me beds were provided but I could bring their personal bedding from home, I noted it would be tough to schlep our queen-size mattress along. They had to make do with the sleep number bed and Egyptian Cotton sheets they were given.

I forgot to ask if they got a flat-screen TV, data ports, or access to a business center. There is free parking.

Let me tell you, the hotel rules are pretty stiff. No late check-outs and no Sunday check-outs. I've gotten discounts for staying over a Saturday night, but never been held hostage on Sunday. Oh, and all guests are asked to conduct themselves in an appropriate manner. In fact, they are quite specific. "Any guests regarded as aggressive and a potential danger to staff and other guests may not be permitted to remain in the hotel." Too many woofs and it's express checkout. Okay, I really get this. The last time I was at the airport Ramada that rule would have evicted the guy who was cracking his girlfriend's noggin against the wall all night.

"All guests will be checked for fleas and ticks at check-in." Again, smart. Many a time I wished that had been done to previous guests before we checked into a flea bag hotel.

"Our guests are provided meals twice daily and always have fresh water available." Do they fill out the little breakfast questionnaire and hang it on the door the night before? Do they tip for room service? And if they drink the bottled water left in their room will there be a charge for it on their bill? Boy, is that one of my hotel pet peeves.

As for my pet's peeves, they didn't have any. They had Special Attention Service for extra socialization, playtime, baths and a nail trim. It sounded so great I almost checked in myself. Gee, maybe they have a rewards program. It turned out to be a world class vacation for the pups.

But just as Paddy started to feel great again, something else happened. The little guy had a bladder stone the size of a peach pit. We saw it on the state-of-the-art x-ray. Owwww. So my dog and my wallet underwent surgery last week. For the record, the dog is fine.

Except he was humiliated by having to wear one of those plastic cones on his head lest he try to gnaw his stitches out. I know it's not polite to laugh, but we all did when Paddy misjudged the amount of room he needed to go through the pet door. Thwaack. Okay, not funny. My baby had a rough time. But he's taking it in stride. The stitches are out, the cone hat is relegated to the closet, and life is good again.

In fact, he is poised to get his 15 minutes of fame when my new book comes out – once again, he's a cover boy. And between his healthy diet and medication, it's been, ummm...a real shot in the arm for him. And for that we're so very, very glad.▼

August 2010

Life happens when you have other plans. That was one of my father's favorite sayings.

On a beautiful Tuesday morning in July, my nearly 92 year old father Mort finished Monday's *N.Y. Times* crossword, called some of the GOP politicians pontificating on TV "schmucks," and started on Tuesday's puzzle.

Then he had a stroke and never regained consciousness, passing away on Sunday night, July 11.

There's really no other way to describe my father Mort than to say he took up a huge amount of space for a small man. He was one of the original *Mad Men*, a television and ad agency art director in the 60s, working for *Vanity Fair*, *Vogue*, then the CBS Network for over 20 years. He was on the team that designed the CBS Eye and launched the Golden Age of TV and promotion for its shows.

Yes, he was generous, impossibly smart, devastatingly funny and loved his family and friends dearly. While he taught me about friendship, responsibility, the New York Yankees and the necessity for good design in all things, including soap dishes and kitchen appliances, I think the greatest lesson he left to me was his theory that nothing that happens in life is so awful if you can get a good story out of it. That theory gave me my writing career and I am thankful for that.

And even his passing, at almost 92 years of age, will doubtless leave us with a story or two to temper the true awfulness of losing him. Just last week he told me that while he was 91 he knew how he was going to get to 95. How? I asked. His answer: "take 684 to 287 and the GW Bridge."

He didn't make 95 but he lived a large 91.There is no chance that a day will go by in my life when I won't think of Mort. I will think of him when I write the story of his last days, surrounded by his adoring and adored wife Joan, his four children, and their spouses.

I will think of him every time I get asked to make a contribution to charity and give as much as I can; whenever I hear Bing Crosby, or music by Gershwin or Cole Porter and expect a quiz on the show its from. I will think of my father every time I drink a dry martini or do a crossword puzzle. I will think of him whenever I'm cold and remember him dismissing my discomfort because after all, be went through the Battle of the Bulge in his summer underwear. Tough to beat that.

I will surely think of him every time I go to purchase a chair, a towel, a lamp, a home appliance – whether he would declare it beautiful or "Boy is that ugly!" He is the only 90 year old I ever knew to spend weeks picking out new window treatments. And the only straight man I know to call the curtains window treatments in the first place.

I will think of him hollering back at the TV when conservative pundits blather. And I will certainly think of him exactly one half hour, like clockwork, after eating his favorite food, a hot dog, and hear his mantra of gastric distress,"I'm sorry I had that hot dog." When I was growing up, that was the family motto.

I will think of Mort whenever the Yankees win and when the bums lose. I will think of him whenever a picture on the wall is crooked, god forbid, and whenever I look in the mirror and hear him say, "That's what you're wearing?" Yes, he could be judgmental and when my self esteem falters I might be having a flashback. But I will also think of how he showed me that people can change and become comfortable with, and then passionate about, things they might not initially understand.

I will think of my father well and often. I miss him terribly already and hope I can continue to tell the stories that prevent life's situations from getting me and the folks around me down. He'd have laughed at the fact that my almost two weeks in NY, between his being stricken, his passing, the funeral and the aftermath left us only eight hours to pack the RV and get ready to leave town for a three week vacation.

Why vacation under the circumstances? We'd rented our house out. He would have enjoyed that hilarious example of "timing is everything" too.

So here I am, on the first leg of a Maine/Canadian vacation in our RV as I write this. It will be a great time for sightseeing and reflection too. In my next column I will report from the road. For now, all I can say is that wherever my father is now, I hope someone asks him if he's comfortable, so he can utter his favorite answer, "I make a living."

He certainly did, In every way.▼

I HAVE QUESTIONABLE CONTENT...WOO-HOO!

For somebody who didn't even know what an app was a few short months ago, it's amazing, but now I am one. That's right, there's an iPhone app, specializing in Gay Rehoboth and apply named Rehomo. It's just been released and I am one of its authors.

Which is hilarious, because if I hadn't been asked to help write an app I probably wouldn't even know what one was. If, like me, you are a technophobe (or tardy adopter compared to the folks who try new stuff right away and are called Early Adopters), here's the skinny: An "app" is shorthand for a software application for today's mobile smart phones. iTunes is an app; so is the CBS news I get on my phone and the addictive bubble breaker game I can't keep my paws off.

Our Rehomo app is kind of a tourist guidebook, like Damron's, or Fodor's but it's written by locals – me and my friend and fellow *Letters from CAMP Rehoboth* writer Rich Barnett. We wanted to make sure it got done locally instead of by some tourism company without a real clue about what to do and where to go and what to see in gay Rehoboth. You get my pick's, Rich's picks, and all the good stuff about Gay Rehoboth.

So how the heck did I, old-fashioned publisher, get to write an app? Rich called me and after he got through tutoring me on twenty first century life, I signed on. We're talking app ground floor here. This was my chance to be avant garde.

Okay, who am I kidding? My idea of avant garde was to finally buy a flat screen TV when everybody else was already investigating 3D. But I hoped this might give me back my cool.

I haven't tried regaining cool since I drove a dune buggy in the Caribbean. But now, instead of getting big clumps of mud in my eye, I get stars in my eyes. After all, I seem to have joined the ranks of (are you ready?) Ellen DeGeneres, Jessica Simpson, and holy, cow, Lady Gaga with having my very own app. I hear there's even an app for translating Sarah Palin's sound bites into English.

Not that I'm going all Gaga, but it feels pretty cool for this old dyke to have some contemporary street cred.

Now, lest you think this is a get-rich-quick scheme, let me fill you in. If you have an iPhone, and iPad or an iPod Touch you can get the Rehomo Beach App for 99 cents from the iTunes store.

Ha! After being split a bunch of ways, this means that in addition to not making a bundle in book publishing, I can now not make a bundle in app publishing. My career is nothing if not consistent.

But, in addition to the street cred, the App even gives me my naughty back. My favorite part of this whole adventure is how long it took us to get authorized by Apple Computer. Rich and I worked on the content and pictures last May and June, sending it off to our partners at Sutro Media in San Francisco, who then sent it along to Apple. Sutro told us it would take from 2 days to two weeks for Apple to review our work and approve it for sale at iTunes and the App stores.

So we waited and waited and waited. Nothing.

Finally, two months later we got the OK. The hold-up? To use Apple's words, "Questionable Content." We had mild references to nudity, alcohol and sex.

Of course we did, this is Rehoboth.

Frankly, I was very proud to have contributed to something with questionable content. Nothing like becoming a renegade the same month you get your first Social Security check.

Of course, then Apple went ahead and approved the app for ages 12 and up, so I guess the nudity and sex references were very mild indeed.

I'm especially excited about sharing opinions about Reho along with my friend Rich. We envision this project the same way: we'd only include stuff we thought was cool and worth seeing, dining at, staying at, etc. In other words, the whole thing would be about expressing our opinions, something I'm good at. And it would be fun, because between Rich and I, we have the market cornered on diverse opinions.

Rich came up with this description and I think it's a hoot:

"This app is the result of a playful collaboration between authors Rich Barnett and Fay Jacobs.

Rich is a 6'3" Southerner. Fay is a 5'3" native New Yorker. She likes to eat out; he prefers to cook in. He drives a pickup truck and she motors about in a BMW. She lives with Schnauzers; he raises roses.

You might think these two writers have nothing in common, but you'd be wrong. Both are storytellers. They chronicle their lives and adventures in Rehoboth Beach, their adopted and beloved hometown, in books, blogs, and magazines (highlighted on this app of course!). And, they like to get together from time to time to hoist a cocktail or two and dream of literary success. She orders a Cosmo; he, a Manhattan."

So there you have it. We've come up with a cool way to promote the things we love about Rehoboth.

So, if you have an iphone or other idevice, check out our Rehomo Beach app. I promise good advice, reviews and, coming soon an updated calendar and even video. And if you don't think it has the right stuff, you can send feedback and we will add some gayboy or dykedrama to suit. For your 99 cents you even get free updates.

And tell your friends with istuff they can learn all about Gayberry RFD.

We're an app by the people, of the people and for the people of Rehomo Beach. An app. I love it and I hope you will too. ▼

August 2010

FAY AND BONNIE'S FABULOUS RV ADVENTURE
(AND WRITER'S RETREAT!)

Hello from Fay and Bonnie's first RV trip in our 27 ft. vehicle, towing a Chevy Tracker, and housing us, our two schnauzers and my computer – so I can vacation while putting finishing touches on my new book, *For Frying Out Loud – Rehoboth Beach Diaries*.

RV life has a learning curve. We drove through Lexington and Concord, Mass. In this case the shot heard 'round the world was Bonnie leaning forward to play with the GPS and accidentally honking the horn with her chest. Oops.

DAY THREE

Lessons: 1. Put Tracker emergency brake on before unhooking to avoid a Bonnie sandwich between car and camper. 2. Keep pliers handy at all times. 3. If you are in the car everything you need is in the camper, or vice versa.

In Salem we saw the Witch House. When they talk about the trials they use it to teach tolerance, including LGBT issues. Yay! In Bah Hahbah we went to our first lobstah pound. Messy, very messy, but good, like a lot of things.

Learned the East Coast's first tourists were called rusticators for the rustic conditions they endured…we are just masticators for all the chewing we are doing.

As RV newbies we don't know where to stow everything. After three days this place looks like a reality TV hoarder episode. And don't even talk to me about the "spaghetti" of wires from laptop, phone charger, iPod, camera charger, oy! I think we are mussticators, not just rusticators.

Tomorrow we are off to Canada, eh, where we are considered official spouses. Unless we consider divorce after trying to hook-up, unhook, level, stow, or otherwise fiddle with all the gear and systems in our traveling circus.

DAY FIVE

Left as early as possible considering all the detaching and complete undoing required. I stand around holding the bag with the pins and chocks and pliers, etc. That's me, left holding the bag. Funny, it's just like my job of being ballast on a boat. Same day, different menial job.

At the border we got the once-over by Canadian feds – they said it was random, but I'm wondering what's in my Homeland Security file. The authorities rifled through everything in the cabin so the place still looks like a rummage sale and further contributed to our messticator status.

Driving through New Brunswick, CA we detoured for construction on Crotch Hill Road (really) along the Bay of Fundy and our GPS (The Bitch on the Dashboard) had a meltdown, sending us the wrong way. Almost caught sunrise at Campobello by mistake. Had lunch in St. Stephens, New Brunswick, the Chocolate Capital of Canada. We sampled, of course.

In St. John, we saw the reverse waterfall...a small falls, where the tidal change comes in and makes it look like the falls runs up. Well, sort of. If you lived in St. John the small ripple would be your big tourist attraction, too.

By the way, the imagined romantic campsite is just a big gravel and crabgrass parking lot. We are side by side by side with dozens of rigs, packed together sardine-style. But after the exhausting day of travel – okay, Bonnie is exhausted, I'm just covered in black and blue paw prints on my thighs from Paddy sitting on my lap and fidgeting for 7 hours. But the GPS conveniently found the liquor store and we are having cocktails inside the RV where it's beautiful.

And if anybody knows where I can get those lights airport workers use to direct airplanes into the gates, please advise.

DAY SEVEN

Headed for the Bay of Fundy and stopped for homemade blueberry ice-cream – it turned out to be $6 for a cone! Good, but single scoop. We did get another scoop, though. The ice-cream crook told us to see St. Martins, a fishing Village with impressive scenery on the Bay of Fundy. I consider the stop six dollars each for tourism advice and a free cone.

The ice-cream Nazi was right. We walked the huge area filled with millions of stones at low tide, and saw giant fishing boats grounded, two stories down from the docks. Bonnie took off her shoes and waded across to some caves, carved by the tides and we both laughed at her navigating her way back over very slippery stones.

Then just hung around waiting for the tide to come back in. I don't think this is what they mean by tidal bore, but...it was like watching paint dry. Then again, like paint, dramatic when done. Had a chowdah suppah while sittin' on the dock of the bay, watching the tide...etc...then, with the car perched on a hill, overlooking the Bay, Schnauzers on our laps, we watched the water return. Peaceful, beautiful, relaxing.

Now working on the book again. Quiet in the RV and a great way to get away from distractions, like blueberry ice cream.

Another lesson. Quiet hours at campsites are generally 10pm-7am. Those hours are not the best time to learn that you have to unlock the cabin of the RV with the key before you open the side door or the alarm will go off. And it's one of those honkin', squeelin', flashin', effin' car alarms you want to rip from the dashboard. See how the lesbians win friends and influence people....

DAY NINE

Off to Nova Scotia. Bonnie spent time unhooking the rig and sewer; I hid inside....

Drove and drove past expanses of absolutely nothing dotted by farms, lakes and additional nothing. Green, pretty. Very few houses and people. Kept driving. Fay and Bonnie went to Nova Scotia and all I got were these lousy hemorrhoids.

Arrived in Halifax for the Pride Parade. Huge! Everyone seemed to come out, if you'll excuse the expression, to watch – gay, straight, families with kids, gay police, firefighters, drag queens, very, very, very cool. The theme was *Free to Be*...and it sure looks like you are that in Halifax. Hah! I've been carded twice this week: once for my Senior Pass to our National Parks and once to get into a gay bar. Irony?

We arrived in tiny Hubbards, NS, set up the RV at the campsite/parking lot, walked the pups to the nearby beach and dined at the Shore Club (since 1946) for one of their famous lobster dinners. The place was a throwback; I expected the Andrews Sisters to pop up any second.

Okay, Nova Scotia is spectacular. We took a drive this morning in part overcast, part drizzle via the Lighthouse Trail along the shore, where the most stunning sight was Peggy's Cove lighthouse atop the incredible outcropping of boulders, nestled in fog and hauntingly beautiful. Reflections and light made for great photos.

Later, we toured Lunenburg and Mahone Bay, lovely, architecturally gorgeous small fishing villages and Blue Rock, a tiny cove that seemed the epitome of the Nova Scotia coast, right down to the lobster traps, colorful buoys, work boats and fishing sheds. Lest I have my city-gal card revoked completely, Bonnie and I donned terminally wrinkled outfits and dined at Fleur de Sel in Lunenburg, one of Canada's top restaurants. Incredible meal, rivaling NY or Paris. The staff was polite enough to ignore the Beverly Hillbillies clothes.

Tonight we "stayed home" for the evening, dining on fish and chips from a stand at the campground – where, although there are empty sites all over, management managed to sandwich us between two families of tenters with small noisy children. This caused small noisy dogs. Oh good, here comes quiet hour and we're in the middle of the reign of terrier. Wish I had a tranquilizer gun. Bribery by doggie biscuit will have to suffice.

DAY WHATEVER

Yeah, just one ugly vista after another here...boats and lighthouses and fishing shacks and....

DAY AFTER WHATEVER

Drove to our campground in Cape Breton. They must be into S&M here because they gave us a ski slope camp site. I put the level on the counter and couldn't find the bubble. We broke out the wood chocks (how much wood could a wood chock chock if a...), put them under the left side tires and backed up onto them. After several tries ("back up, no, go forward, STOP, you're not back far enough, oh, shit") we went inside for martinis. It was like cocktails on the Titanic. Darn, we had to have chowder, clams and mussels again tonight. This writer's life is tough.

SOMETIME IN JULY
THE CAPE BRETON ROLLER COASTER

Drove the famous 8-hour Cabot trail loop, Schnauzers in the back seat (Dog is my co-pilot). Once again, crummy weather, with fog and drizzle. While photo ops suffered, we loved the roller coaster ride along the very edge of the sea, up high in the mountains, then plunging to incredible valleys, twisting, turning on the narrow road, overlooking spectacular cliffs and mountain ranges, fishing villages, seafood restaurants and pottery, glass, leather, basket weaving and tchotchke artisans. Amazing vistas I cannot even attempt to describe. See it someday if you can.

As for RV life, I'm loving it. Bonnie was terrified I'd spook at some point and demand to be taken to a Holiday Inn Express. No such thing. The book is going well, and I adore working in the RV. At a certain point we stopped caring if our clothes matched and started to look like vagrants. Will work for lobster.

THE NEXT DAY

Moxie, Paddy and I watched Bonnie do all that butch stuff on this morning, getting the rig ready to head out. Just as we started to roll along a cabinet in the RV opened and I went to the back to close it. That's when we hit the pothole and I went flying into the wall. I feel like I've been knee-capped by the Sopranos. And with a bulging bruise on my head, if I was a quarterback I'd be benched. In fact, much like my former boating days, bruises are us. From now on I try to stay put in the shotgun seat while moving.

WILD MOOSE CHASE

What the heck did we do to piss off Mother Nature? Drizzle and fog again. If Bonnie hadn't worn a Gorton's Yellow slicker I would have lost her entirely.

Spent the morning in Louisbourg at a meticulously re-created 18th century fortress. Purportedly, the fortress was surrounded on three sides by ocean, but you could have fooled us. Okay, sometimes I heard waves.

But the historic site, complete with re-enactors, cannon blasts, and a working bakery and farm, was mercifully free of crass commercialism and we really enjoyed the exhibits. On the way back to the campsite we drove two more hours on that damn Cabot trail and still no moose sightings, despite Moose Crossing signs everywhere. If the moose is loose, where is he?

We headed to dinner at a local Distillery and Inn when GPS bitch told us to turn left onto a skinny unpaved road. I said "no," but my adventurous mate overruled me. First it was gravel, then dirt, then mud with grass growing between tire tracks, then muddy ruts, deep puddles, and finally massive axle-threatening sink holes. Dark forest beckoned on either side, no signs of life, moose or otherwise, as we bucked forward, deeper and deeper into the mire. I panicked. No bars on the cell phone. We'll get stuck, blow a tire! It's getting dark, My God, all they'll find of us will be bones and golf clubs. Turn around! Turn around!

Bonnie, of course was not rattled. Then the dashboard moron said "Continue 11 miles." Hell, twenty minutes into this mess we'd only gone a mile and a half. Whether it was 11 more or 40, the outcome seemed identical – they'd find us sometime in April.

Finally, Bonnie agreed to u-turn (no easy task) and we retreated, our teeth and the car's chassis ratting as we bounced and banged and crept our way back to the main road. The only sign we saw on the way said *SLOW*. We howled.

And when we got to the distillery, we partook.

And of course, do you think we saw any moose?

AUGUST 1

We arrived in Truro, NS, mid-province, last night, staying at the nicest campground yet, with actual trees between campsites. Downtown wasn't much except some nicely restored homes and more than a dozen cool wooden sculptures carved from the remains of trees which succumbed to Dutch Elm Disease. Lemonade from lemons.

Passed through Bible Hill, NS and I loved their town branding: *Bible Hill – a progressive community*. Given the name of the town, I guess they had to go with something like that. Glad tourism there isn't my job.

This morning we dined at Sugar Moon Maple Farm, a cute little restaurant at the end of a long winding dirt road, where we were greeted by a rainbow sticker on the door, friendly staff and a table full of women of a certain age breakfasting there as well. We'd found our people. Had terrific pancakes with freshly made maple syrup, maple sausage, maple baked beans and maple whipped cream atop coffee. We're lucky that Paddy is still the only one in the family with diabetes.

Baked beans for breakfast. I'm feeling a little Paul Bunyanish.

And then, after breakfast we saw the moose. Sadly it was in a nature preserve Bonnie dragged me to because she was sick of my anguish over herds of missing moose. There, in a large field was a big old moose with his lovely moose wife. What a rack, as they say – on him, not her. And Mr. Moose came right up to me, stared me in the eye and...sneezed. God bless him, the big brown beast. I can leave Canada tomorrow a happy camper, having seen my chocolate moose.

TUESDAY, AUGUST 2, PERHAPS

Made the long drive yesterday back across the boring highway in Nova Scotia to New Brunswick, got to see the reversing falls for a second time (woo-hoo) and crossed back into the U.S. to Calais, ME. Situated near the border of a bilingual country, I assumed the name of the city was pronounced a la francais (Ca-lay), but no, it is pronounced like what happens to your hands when you do too much manual labor, not that I'd know.

Met our friend Alan and his partner Kent for dinner. Do you know that TV reality show, the *Fabulous Beekman Boys* about the two New York gay guys who buy a farm and fight all the time? It should be called the Fabulous Bicker Boys. I don't give those reality boys another month. I mention this because Kent is a farmer and now he and Alan are the real life gay farmers, much more real than reality TV. Oh yeah, more lobster. Good thing for bibs; clean clothes running low.

In fact, for the first time in 40 years I experienced a Laundromat. Nothing has changed. I still had to search in the sofa for quarters to slide in the slots. Four decades later it's exactly the same, only this time, mercifully, I wasn't washing mini-skirts. (Oy, I'm having a college flashback, complete with Mateus wine and bellbottoms).

Then we drove several hours across middle of nowhere Maine, stopping for a good but greasy Italian sub in the town of Passagassawakeag. There's nothing I can say more amusing than the lunch menu in concert with the name of the town.

Finally! Our campsite in Wells, ME is the kind I'd always pictured. Large wooded sites, turned so your neighbor's rig is not in your face. Gorgeous. And there was a path to the water where Bonnie and I, along with Moxie and Paddy sat in Adirondack chairs, sipping Bacardi Sangria (black cherry soda for adults), overlooking a wide, rocky-coasted bay.

Then, tonight I simply fell in love with Camden, ME with its busy, beautiful harbor, historic buildings, shops and galleries I cannot afford and a mean bowl of clam chowder. Ahhhhhh.

AUGUST 3, I THINK

Okay, Uncle. We just came from the 63rd Annual Maine Lobster Festival in Rockland, ME. Crafts, artisans, music, snacks from all the worst food groups, and lobster everything – shirts, hats, pajamas, recipes etc. Bonnie and I exited the giant Eating Tent having consumed four scrumptious lobsters between us. But I believe we have finally OD'd...somebody get me a hamburger, stat!

AUGUST 6

I see gay people! Rainbows abound in Ogunquit, Maine, our last stop on this whistle-stop tour. Another beautiful Maine town, but with a queer bent. Hooray!

Went fishing and Bonnie is irritated because I caught a fish and she didn't. I reminded her we should both be irritated since the resulting filet was pretty much a $108 McDonald's fish sandwich. But the boat ride was waaaay fun.

Heading home, with my book finished(!), a bus filled with souvenirs and newly purchased RV accessories we didn't know we needed, plus heads filled with plans for future trips. Look for our rig, The Bookmobile, coming soon to a town near you! ▼

September 2010

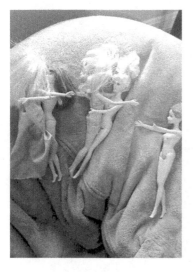

Recently, a lesbian friend showed me a photo she got from her married daughter. There were five Barbie Dolls on a blanket. Two pairs of Barbies lay tangled in hot embraces and the fifth, had outstretched arms, as if to say "What about me?" The display was staged by a four year old.

Now it goes to my point about change, that Mom didn't flinch and even added the text "Hmmmmm...I have no words." Grandma just laughed.

That incident was followed the next day by an episode of *Rizzoli and Isles*, the new cop show with Angie Harmon and Sasha Alexander solving brutal murders. In this case, a lesbian wearing a wedding ring was killed outside a Boston club. As the police do in most murder investigations, they suspected the spouse first. "Think it's the wife?" one cop said to the other. Only as far as I can tell, this was the first time mainstream TV has matter-of-factly included a same sex Massachusetts wife as a matter-of-fact suspect.

To solve the crime, Angie Harmon went undercover at the gay bar. What could have been a field day for snarky homophobic innuendo, simply wasn't. The scene was tasteful, hilarious, and the best part (spoiler alert, if you haven't watched this one yet), was the discovery that wifey did do it, so frankly, we're being treated just like everyone else...huzzah!

On the big screen change has come by way of Angelina Jolie in *Salt*. I know she's not playing for our team, but in this frenetic spy film she does the same butch action hero stuff as any given James Bond. She leaps from windows, lands on moving vehicles and positively kicks butt. It's a lipstick lesbian fantasy if ever there was one, and that her behavior is acceptable to all speaks volumes about the new normal for the role of women, gay or otherwise.

We've come a long way, baby, judging by the way women were treated in the 60s and shown on TV's *Mad Men*, the drama about New York's Madison Avenue advertising business. We see agency execs gulp booze in the office and engage in rabid ogling of their secretaries. In that culture, women were grossly disrespected and consistently denied opportunity. Their simmering rage finally touched off the feminist bonfire.

And Angelina Joile in *Salt* is the apex of feminism.

"It doesn't get any more equal than that," said one of six post-feminist lesbians sitting at my dining room table last week, recalling the quaint phrase "women's lib" and the forty-year evolution of women's rights.

"Remember those consciousness raising sessions – you know, where everybody got a mirror and looked at their own body parts?"

"Did that actually happen? I think it was a myth, like burning bras."

"Well, Gloria Steinem must have done it."

"My god, there's no way I could do that today, my body won't bend that way."

"I'd need a forklift to get back up."

"Can you see us all in the emergency room trying to explain what happened?"

I laughed so hard I had to leave the room and readers of a certain age know why.

The conversation then turned to the film *The Kids Are All Right*, starring Julianne Moore and Annette Bening.

Now Annette Bening is my one dispensation. If you are coupled, do you have a celebrity monogamy dispensation? My spouse of 28-plus years would wink and look the other way if I had the chance to um…go out on a date with Annette Bening. Like that's gonna happen. But the dispensation has been offered and accepted, just in case hell should freeze over.

But I digress.

The Kids Are All Right, is an honest depiction of a very contemporary long-term lesbian relationship. Annette and Julianne play characters who love each other but are navigating a rough patch. Their son seeks out his sperm donor father and the story turns hilarious and insightful, examining a marriage being tested, tried and ultimately (well, I won't say…).

What's fun, and very encouraging, is that author-director Lisa Cholodenko did not shy away from showing a dysfunctional gay family, thereby proving exactly how equal we can be to a family suffering heterosexual dysfunction.

But my favorite clue that the film signals change is that Cholodenko was not afraid to piss off lesbian audiences (I am side-stepping a spoiler here) by having the plot take a turn lots of people might have wished it hadn't. That being said, Julianne Moore's final speech is so magical, and the perform- ances so stunning and fun (way to go, Annette!), the film works for many, many satisfying reasons.

All this being said, I closed my eyes the other night, hopeful that things are improvinig for gay people, with the country coming around (albeit slowly) to the concept of equality for all, including gay marriage equality.

What was I thinking? By morning, I learned that tea- bagging, gay baiting, coven-joining, reparative therapy- endorsing right-wing nut bag Christine O'Donnell had won the Republican Nomination to run for the Senate in Delaware. I wanted to hurl. Not only do her politics and ethics offend me (she's been illegally living on campaign funds) but as an editor I'm aghast – she makes up words. Today's was "factuous," as in "those claims are not factuous." Yesterday she said "The United States is the free-est place in the country." And she thinks we're not worthy?

In bad news to worse, a local Aryan Nation organization (yes, there is one here) marched for White Power on the shore this weekend.

So I'm trying to hang onto the two steps forward, one step back theory to keep my sanity, but it's tough. I close my eyes and fanatisize Angelina Jolie swooping down on those hate-filled Aryan marchers and kicking the living daylights out of them. And while she's busy, maybe *Rizolli and Isles* can get Christine O'Donnell into an interrogation room to confess about the root of her raging homophobia.

And oh yeah, while all that's going on, maybe Annette Bening and I can sneak away for a martini.

I can dream, can't I?▼

Afterword

Hello, readers. A lot has happened since this book was first published.

My four books *As I Lay Frying, Fried & True, For Frying Out Loud,* and *Time Fries* were all originally published by A&M Books, a successor to the legendary Naiad Press. Readers of a certain age may recall that Naiad was formed in 1974, by four courageous lesbians. Two of the women—Anyda Marchant, a lesbian novelist who wrote under the name Sarah Aldridge, and her partner and editor Muriel Crawford—lived in Rehoboth Beach.

Naiad Press was the first and became, in its day, the most successful lesbian publishing company in the world. Of course, in the 70s you couldn't even buy a lesbian novel in a bookstore. You had to mail order and it arrived like pornography in a plain brown wrapper. That's how it was marketed— we'll send it to you and nobody has to know. No wonder it took us so long to feel any pride.

In 1995, Anyda and Muriel left Naiad Press and, though by this time in their eighties, founded A&M Books of Rehoboth. It was Anyda who suggested I compile my published newspaper columns into my first book. Anyda and Muriel were brave women and fierce feminists. They were Rehoboth's Gertrude Stein and Alice B. Toklas. They loved each other, publishing and Scotch whisky, not necessarily in that order. When Anyda and Muriel, a couple for 57 years, both passed away in 2005, I became owner of A&M Books. And I tried, the best I could, to live up to their example—in literature and cocktails.

It was great fun but not easy running a small independent publishing house—literally; it was my house. The shed was the Rehoboth book depository, my spouse was fulfillment manager, and my Schnauzer worked security.

Now, after a decade as a publisher, I am thrilled to have merged A&M Books with the wonderful publisher Bywater Books. The entire *Frying* series has been given new life in beautifully produced editions, along with another A&M book called *The Carousel* by Stefani Deoul. And most importantly, Anyda and Muriel, the original publishers will continue to be celebrated as the true pioneers they were.

And, for a retiree, my life is suddenly going in all kinds of surprising new directions and I'm having a blast. I still live in Rehoboth Beach, still write my columns, and still have wacky experiences that are worth the story I can tell. The march toward equality alone has been worth reams of paper and barrels of ink.

With running a publishing house off my plate, I was free to do the second most exciting thing that has happened to me. At age 60-something, I have a whole new career. I'm touring with my oral memoir *Aging Gracelessly: 50 Shades of Fay.* Reviewers have called the reading "sit-down comedy" as I tell some fun stories from my books and chart our LGBT march from the closeted outlaw days to marriage equality. As I write this I am headed to The Big Apple and the Duplex Cabaret Theatre on Christopher Street in NYC. For this lapsed New Yorker it will be a huge thrill.

So please, check out all of my new Bywater Books editions and come see *50 Shades of Fay* if I show up in a venue near you.

And remember, nothing is ever so horrible if it's worth the story you can tell!

Fay Jacobs
April, 2016
Rehoboth Beach, DE

PRAISE FOR FAY JACOBS

"Her columns... are laugh out loud funny and the best part is that Jacobs is sincere...those who enjoy her essays won't be disappointed and those reading her for the first time will understand why she's such a beloved columnist." —*Lambda Literary Review*

"It's an intelligent, hysterically funny and occasionally poignant look at how we live today, with hopes for tomorrow. Recommended for everyone, male or female, gay or straight. Five stars out of five." —*Echo Magazine*

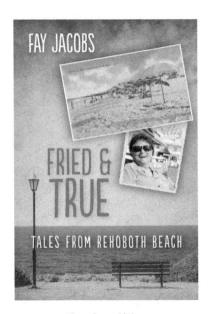

As I Lay Frying
Print 978-1-61294-071-7
Ebook 978-1-61294-072-4

Fried and True
Print 978-1-61294-073-1
Ebook 978-1-61294-074-8

Bywater BOOKS

www.bywaterbooks.com

"Fay's essays resonate with warmth, candid hmor, and the unabashed joy of finding one's place." — *OUTtraveler*

"Fay Jacob's hilarious dispatches are funny, touching—and real. This is a true laugh riot, as Fay wittily takes on sexuality, politics, relationships, and day-to-day dilemmas." —*Insight Out Book Club*

Fay Jacobs' books are part memoir, part social commentary, and an easy and fun summer read. Very smart, very funny, very insightful. These books will appeal to everyone.
— *Northampton's Pride and Joy Bookstore*

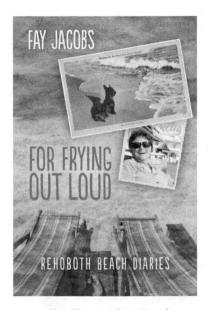

For Frying Out Loud
Print 978-1-61294-075-5
Ebook 978-1-61294-076-2

Time Fries!
Print 978-1-61294-077-9
Ebook 978-1-61294-078-6

www.bywaterbooks.com

At Bywater Books we love good books about lesbians just like you do, and we're committed to bringing the best of contemporary lesbian writing to our avid readers. Our editorial team is dedicated to finding and developing outstanding writers who create books you won't want to put down.

We sponsor the Bywater Prize for Fiction to help with this quest. Each prize winner receives $1,000 and publication of their novel. We have already discovered amazing writers like Jill Malone, Sally Bellerose, and Hilary Sloin through the Bywater Prize. Which exciting new writer will we find next?

For more information about Bywater Books and the annual Bywater Prize for Fiction, please visit our website.

www.bywaterbooks.com

Printed in the USA
CPSIA information can be obtained
at www.ICGtesting.com
JSHW022323140824
68134JS00019B/1256